PLAYS FOR HOLIDAYS

BY BILL MOORE

Library of Congress Cataloging-in-Publication Data

Moore, Bill, 1930-
Plays for holidays / by Bill Moore.
p. cm.
Contents: Decision time — The scourge of scars — Love: the greatest power — A mother's love — Monuments of success — Remembering father — In a foreign land — The bottom line — One life for another — First things first — The good old days — The road to Bethlehem
ISBN 0-87403-853-7
1. Holidays—Drama. I. Title.
PS3563.0584P56 1991
812'.54—dc20 91-7304
CIP

Edited by Theresa C. Hayes

CONTENTS

INTRODUCTION

The purpose of these skits is to enrich our spiritual lives. Each play focuses on one holiday in order to examine the greater significance of that day. In this manner, holidays can become a time for Christian reflection, not simply another day off work.

Settings for these plays include common locations such as homes, churches, offices, restaurants, and TV shows. Hopefully, members of your audience will recognize their own personal thoughts, actions, and weaknesses. If they do, they may gain significant insights into Christian living, recognize their many blessings, realize scriptural road-markers along their own spiritual journeys, and above all, gain new hope for every day.

Suggestions for simple props, costumes, and stage settings are provided with each script. Printed programs describing each setting will allow you to avoid elaborate backgrounds.

The plays may be altered to fit the particular needs of any size church group and most ages. They may also be read in readers' theatre style, possibly to be followed by a group discussion.

The length of presentation varies from thirty to forty-five minutes.

Decision Time

Characters
Gerald Romano; TV personality a là Geraldo Revera
Lisa O'Hara; college student, sensitive, dressed informally
Dale Brown; businessman, assertive, caring, age 40 to 50's
Helen Brown; businesswoman, also assertive and caring age 40 to 50's
Three characters in audience who ask questions

Scenes

The stage is split between two settings. On one side is a TV-show setting. A large sign identifying the "Gerald Romano Show" hangs on the wall. On the other side of the stage is a kitchen setting.

Scene 1: TV talk show, New Year's Day
Scene 2: Flashback to family kitchen
Scene 3: Back to TV talk show

Props

Kitchen table with cups, two chairs on other side
Cordless microphone, or facsimile
Three chairs on one side of stage
Sign: Gerald Romano Show
Newspapers

Performance Tips

Use lights to signal scene changes, dimming the lights on the TV setting and bringing them up on the kitchen, and vice versa.

To provide local impact, use names of your hometown, local mall, etc. when indicated.

Scene One: *The play opens on the* TV *side with* Dale *and* Lisa *seated.*

Gerald (*walks to front centerstage, and uses a microphone to address the audience*): Welcome to the Gerald Romano Show! Today's show is special because of the unique tradition practiced by many of us on New Year's Day. I am speaking, of course, of the practice of making New Year's resolutions. As we shall see, this tradition affords a special opportunity for Christians to make life-changing decisions.

Day-to-day decisions come in all sizes, and can be very simple or very complex. Today we will see how some quickly-made decisions resulted in life-and-death situations for the people involved.

Here with us, we have two people who risked their lives to save the lives of total strangers. May I introduce our guests. (*Points to Lisa*): This is Lisa O'Hara, a senior at (nearest Christian) College in (state). (*Lisa nods.*)

And this (*points*) is Dale Brown, a public accountant who lives here in (city). (*Dale nods.*)

The lives of these two people are deeply interwoven. One year ago today, they both risked their lives to save the life of a total stranger. Dale saved a little boy, and a few minutes later, Lisa saved Dale's life. As a result, she received the National Good Samaritan Award this past month. That's when we first learned about their story. What compelled each of these people to risk their lives so that a total stranger might live? Today we hope to find some answers to that question. (*Turns to Dale*): Tell us about your accident last year.

Dale: I was returning home from a business trip to (nearby town), driving along (street). Ahead of me, the road made a sharp turn at the edge of the (local) River. Just as I reached the turn, a small boy jumped out from behind a parked car onto the street right in front of me.

Gerald: And you were faced with a potential disaster.

Dale (*nods*): I had only two options. If I jerked the car to the left to avoid hitting the child, I would smash head-on into the guardrail over the river. If I didn't turn away, he would be killed.

Gerald: Which option did you choose?

Dale: I slammed on my brakes, swerved to the left, and smashed head-on into the guardrail. From that moment on, I don't remember a thing.

Gerald: And that's how you ended up in the river?

Dale (*nods*): I was more concerned about saving that boy's life than what might happen to me. I just thank God I did the right thing.

Gerald: The question in my mind, and I'm sure what the audience would like to know, is—why? Why did you risk your life for that child?

Dale: For the first few months following the accident, I asked myself that same question. Since my reaction was instantaneous—there was no time to think—my decision must have been due to the presence of God in my life; a force beyond my power to control. That's the only explanation that makes any sense to me.

Gerald: Would you elaborate on that for us?

Dale: It's a difficult thing to explain. I guess I would call it, "spiritual guidance."

Gerald: So that our audience might better understand, would you tell us how spiritual guidance affects your life?

Dale: In the Bible, Jesus tells us that we will receive spiritual help to face our daily problems. And that means *all* problems—not just life-and-death emergencies.

Gerald: At what point in your life did you make the decision to completely rely upon that spiritual guidance?

Dale: That decision took place twenty years ago today—on New Year's Day. That's when my wife and I made the unforgettable, life-changing choice to obey the Lord. If we hadn't made that choice, I'm convinced that little boy would have been killed. It was either *him*, or *me*. And I'm certain my *natural* survival instincts would have prevented me from swerving to avoid him.

Gerald: Thank you for that explanation. (*Person in audience raises hand. Gerald sees, walks to person, extends microphone.*)

Person #1 (*stands, speaks*): Mr. Brown, did you experience any panic when you first noticed that boy?

Dale (*shakes head*): No, I didn't.

Person #1: Weren't you afraid you would be killed?

Dale (*shakes head*): I didn't think about it. All I can figure is that my resolve had something to do with my Christian beliefs. No matter when my final day arrives, I have faith that Heaven is a place of rest and peace—and I am going there. However, I did not have time to think this through at the moment—I just reacted. (*Person #*1 *nods and sits down.*)

Gerald: When did you find out what happened after you struck that guardrail?

Dale: After I regained consciousness, one of the nurses at the hospital told me what had happened. In fact, she saved the newspaper account and gave it to me.

Gerald: Did you find out who rescued you?

Dale (*shakes head*): Not until you called last week. The newspaper reported only that the rescuer left the scene before the officers learned her name.

Gerald: And now you've had a chance to meet the person who put *her* life on the line so that *you* might live.

Dale (*turns toward* Lisa *excited*LY): In the few minutes we had together before this show started, I couldn't begin to express to you the depth of gratitude I feel for your heroic efforts; I owe my life to you!

Gerald: Now let's hear from Lisa. (*To her*): Would you tell us, please,what led to your involvement in this accident?

Lisa: I was returning to school from my parents' home in (city in another state) after the Christmas holiday. I was following another car. (*Gestures to Dale*): As it turned out, he was the other driver. (*To audience*): When I saw that boy run into the street, I instantly hit my brakes. The other driver quickly swerved and slammed head-on through the guardrail. I'll never forget that terrible moment. The car rolled end-over-end into the (local) River.

Gerald: Tell us what happened then.

Lisa: I slid to a stop, jumped out, and ran to the guardrail. The car was half-submerged in chunks of ice on the river. The windshield was smashed and the car was slowly filling with water and sinking. There was no sign of life.

Gerald: What did you do then?

Lisa: At first I was too stunned to even think. I recall crying out, "Please God! Help me! What can I do?" The answer came as quickly as a thought, "Try to save the driver's life." I ran back to my car and grabbed my life jacket—

Gerald (*interrupting*): Do you keep a life jacket in your car?

Lisa: No. My parents had just given me one as a Christmas gift. You see, my friends and I do a lot of canoeing.

Gerald: What an amazing coincidence!

Lisa: I'd rather think of it as God's providential care. As I pulled on the life jacket, I noticed the little boy staring at me—practically in shock. I yelled to him to go find someone call the emergency squad. When he took off, I ran down the bank toward the car and jumped in. I swam out and grabbed the door handle. It seemed like it took a long time to get the door open! Then I unhooked the driver's seat belt and pulled him out of the car.

Gerald: Was there any sign of consciousness?

Lisa (*shakes head*): None. But there was a lot of blood. I was afraid he was gone. I swam with him toward the shore, trying to keep his head above water. When we finally got to the bank, I found he wasn't breathing, so I rolled him over to drain some of the water out of his lungs. Then I started mouth-to-mouth resuscitation. (*Excitedly*): And he started breathing again! I'll treasure that moment as long as I live! A few minutes later, the rescue squad arrived.

Gerald: And they took over from there?

Lisa (*nods*): Yes, they immediately rushed him to the hospital.

Gerald: And thanks to your speedy action, he wasn't in that freezing water long enough to develop hypothermia.

Lisa (*nods*): There is one other fact about this experience that amazes me yet today; I took a thirty-mile detour from my usual route back to school! I wanted to take a look at the (local) River to see if it would be a good spot for canoeing !

Gerald: And if you hadn't taken that route, you wouldn't have been there to rescue Dale at all! What an amazing coincidence! But why did you leave the accident scene without giving anyone your name? The National Good Samaritan Award Committee spent several months trying to locate you. You missed out on a lot of publicity by leaving the area!

Lisa (*smiles*): Well, to be perfectly truthful, I was freezing to death at the time! I wasn't thinking about publicity! Besides, I just did what I felt was necessary.

Gerald: Now for the big question; why *did* you risk your life?

Lisa: For the same reason as Mr. Brown—because my Christian faith teaches me to have a deep concern for helping others any way I can.

Gerald: And that's your reason for plunging into that freezing water to save his life?

Lisa (*nods*): Yes, that and one other fact that played a big part in my becoming a Christian in the first place.

Gerald: And what would that be?

Lisa: When I was a child, I almost died from neglect. However, a dedicated Christian couple had organized a group from their church to help needy children and families. The very day they heard about me, they found a home for me with a loving family.

Gerald: What do you remember about your problems?

Lisa: Not much at all. I was only four at the time. I was later told that my natural parents had died, and that I was living in the worst possible poverty conditions—close to starvation. The couple that took me in later adopted me. Then, a few months later, Dad changed jobs and we moved from the community.

Gerald: How did that early experience influence your decision to try to save Dale's life?

Lisa: Because of the faith of the people who reached out to me and saved my life, I also became a Christian. Their actions were straight out of Matthew, chapter twenty-five.

Gerald: Would you tell the audience what that chapter says?

Lisa: It contains one of the most important messages in the Bible. In it, Jesus is telling us about helping the "least" of the human race, specifically the naked and hungry. And I qualified on both points! That couple stepped right in and saved my life. From them, I learned a vital lesson: never pass up an opportunity to help others in need. And he (*points to* Dale) was in desperate need in that river!

Gerald: Thank you, Lisa.

(*Person in audience raises hand. Gerald sees hand, walks to person, extends microphone.*)

Person #2 (*stands, speaks*): What you did was extremely dangerous. Weren't you afraid you might die?

Lisa (*shakes head*): No, I wasn't. I learned to swim at an early age, and am not afraid of deep water.

Person #2: I know how to swim, too, but there's no way I'd ever leap into an ice-filled river. That would be like committing suicide!

Lisa: Two other factors influenced my decision: I've had training in life-saving skills and I'm a Christian. My decision to follow Jesus means being obedient to Him and using my skills and energy on His behalf even when—perhaps *especially* when—the situation might threaten my own comfort level. Without that commitment, I probably wouldn't have done what I did. (*Person #2 sits down.*)

Gerald: What are your plans for after you graduate?

Lisa: I've spent a lot of time praying about that. I've decided to go into Christian education, primarily to work with children from poor families. This could take the shape of mission projects in either the United States, or some foreign country.

Gerald: Your early life experiences must have had a big impact upon your decision.

Lisa (*nods*): In addition to living in extreme poverty, I've learned that my natural parents were both illiterate, and my father was an unemployed alcoholic. He regularly assaulted both me and my mother. From what I've learned in college and from others, I'm convinced that poverty has a terrible impact upon children—especially infants.

Gerald: And you have decided to meet that challenge.

Lisa (*nods*): Well, hopefully, a small part of it! I want to spend my life sharing Christ's love with children. Just like my adoptive parents did for me. Theirs was truly Christian love in action.

Gerald: That was a beautiful story, Lisa. (*To Dale*): Earlier, when I asked you to explain "spiritual guidance," you said something about a life-changing decision you and your wife made many years ago. Would you explain what happened?

Dale (*looks up, reflecting*): Our new life in Christ started on New Year's morning twenty years ago. My wife and I were sitting in our kitchen reading the newspaper. I'll never forget our discussion! Our decision that morning has had a dramatic affect on our lives right up to the present time.

Lights go down on the TV *stage.*

END OF SCENE ONE.

SCENE TWO: D*ale moves to the kitchen setting, and joins* Helen *who enters from the wings. They sit leisurely at the table sipping coffee or juice and scanning different sections of the newspaper. To make it easy to read the newspaper aloud, tape copies of the appropriate sections of this play to the inside of the newspaper.*

Helen and Dale *enjoy the silence for a few seconds after the lights come up, before* Helen *speaks.*

Helen: I really enjoy these lazy New Year's mornings. . . get up when we want to. . . no boss to answer to.

Dale (*looks up*): I totally agree. Just sit back and relax.

Helen (*laughs*): The only problem with New Year's Day is that we need to make resolutions for this coming year.

Dale: The ones we made last year were right on target.

Helen: Right! We reduced our church donations, dropped our contribution to the city relief fund, and voted against all tax levies. That *really* cut down expenses!

Dale (*excited*): And we invested the money we saved in the stock market. (*Slaps hand to table.*) The best investments we've ever made!

Helen: We really had no other choice. We were forced to make a drastic cutback in our spending. As I recall, we only grossed around $78,000 from both of our jobs last year.

Dale: We just did what we had to do.

Helen: And it really paid off. We also made enough money on our stocks to buy a new RV and a boat!

Dale (*grins*): Do you remember what Pastor Edwards said after we started taking those weekend boat trips with our friends?

Helen (*nods, laughs*): I'll never forget it! He said he missed us at church and reminded us that we need to keep Sunday for the Lord. That's when I told him we can worship just as easily on our boat as in church. (*Chuckles.*) I didn't tell him the truth: that we always sleep in on Sunday mornings following our all-night parties with friends. (*Laughs.*)

Dale (*chuckles*): And then he said something about the church needing a steadier flow of donations to meet the budget. I felt like telling him, "It's a pay-as-you-go thing. When we go to church—we pay." (*Both laugh.*)

Helen: And every time we did attend, he mentioned that the church's community outreach fund was the one used to help homeless and needy people. I'm glad they finally scrapped that program altogether!

Dale: It was a total waste of money. All those people really need is to find a job and stick with it.

Helen: I agree. It sure would cut down on welfare costs. (*Points to an article in the paper.*) Here's a summary of last expenses. (*Reads aloud.*) "Welfare fraud convictions reached an all-time high last year, costing taxpayers (use dollar figure appropriate for your community) in lost appropriations." (*Looks at Dale*): The only way to cut down stealing from taxpayers is to eliminate *all* government programs.

Dale (*nods*): As I've always said, "God helps those who help themselves."

Helen (*nods*): That's all it takes—a decision to step out and find a job. (*Chuckles.*) They could start today—with New Year's resolutions.

Dale: After seeing what our resolutions did for us last year, I can't think of any changes we need to make.

Helen: I agree. If we just stick to our plan, we should come out on top again. We might even add a deck out back with a hot tub overlooking our enclosed pool.

Dale: Great idea! I'll see if I can find an ad on decks. (*Picks up paper, scans through it, suddenly stops, shocked*): Do you remember that article in yesterday's paper about the little girl who was found in an alley here in town?

Helen (*nods angrily*): I certainly do! Her parents should be punished for permitting her to live like that! They're probably on welfare!

Dale (*reads from paper*): "Officer Callahan learned that the girl had climbed into a dumpster, eaten some food scraps, then crawled under a pile of newspapers to keep warm in the freezing temperatures. 'She was nothing but skin and bones when I found her,' Callahan stated. 'She was wearing only a torn summer blouse and shorts.'"

Helen (*shocked*): That's terrible!

Dale (*continues reading*): "I looked in the dumpster because I thought I had heard something. Then I saw a bare foot sticking out beneath a pile of newspapers. I quickly pulled her out and rushed her to the hospital."

Helen: Thank God he saw her! How's she doing now?

Dale (*reads*): "At the present time, she is responding well to treatment."

Helen (*relieved*): I'm so glad to hear that.

Dale (*continues reading*): "He later learned that the child's parents were killed in an accident three months ago and she was now living with her grandmother. Upon arriving at that address, Callahan found the elderly woman in a coma. He rushed her to (   ) Hospital, where doctors determined that she had suffered a stroke a few days earlier. Her condition is still critical." (*Points to paper, shocked*): That's where they lived! It looks like a doghouse! (*Shows her the picture.*)

Helen (*speaks in choked voice*): That was their home? That's terrible! No bathroom, heat or even electricity. How could that possibly happen right here in our community? That poor little girl didn't have a chance!

Dale (*reads paper*): "One official stated, 'The agencies that would normally have helped were unable to assist this family due to the failure of the tax levies and the decrease in contributions to charitable programs. Members of our community have sent the clear message that they don't care what happens to children born into poverty. And what's even worse, the only church that had provided emergency funds for many years was forced to drop the program due to lack of donations. It makes you wonder what has happened to Christian love and support in our community.'"

Both are stunned, sit silently for several seconds, Dale with hand to his forehead, Helen with head bowed.

Helen (*barely able to talk*): We voted down those levies. And we dropped our support for the city relief fund.

Dale (*speaks in choked voice*): And that was our church that dropped the outreach program.

Helen (*shakes head*): I can't believe it. *Our* decisions helped cause the failure of both of the levies, and the church program. (*Wipes eyes.*)

Dale: I can't believe what we've done. (*Choked voice*): That little girl—no one to care for her, no food or clothes, and no real home. (*Drops head into hands.*) I feel so guilty.

Helen (*weeps*): All of those decisions we made last New Year's Day were so selfish! How could we be so heartless?

Dale (*bows head, prays*): Please, Lord, forgive us. We didn't know what we were doing. It's the worst thing we've ever done.

Helen (*bows head*): What we can do, Lord? Please help us!

END OF SCENE TWO

SCENE THREE: *Lights come up on TV show setting. Dale has returned.*

Dale: Thank God our prayers were answered! Both of our lives were drastically changed.

Gerald: Was that New Year's Day the first time you recognized the need for spiritual guidance in your life?

Dale: No. Back in high school I made the decision to accept and to follow Jesus—whatever that required. I took my commitment very seriously in everything I did—school, church activities, and later on, my job and marriage.

Gerald: Did your wife have a similar commitment?

Dale (*nods*): Yes, she did, although her decision came a few years later.

Gerald: Well, what happened to your decisions to follow Christ?

Dale: During the first five years of our marriage, our motivation for maintaining a solid spiritual life slowly eroded. We were gradually caught up in society's race to grab all the money you can, go for the exciting life, never mind those who are suffering. Before long, we had lost all interest in spiritual things.

Gerald: Until that unforgettable New Year's Day.

Dale (*nods*): That was an extremely difficult moment. We were confronted head-on by the results of our selfish, greedy life-style. Our interest was focused entirely on things like replacing our five-year-old RV and spending weekends boating on (local) Lake. (*Person in audience raises hand.*)

Gerald walks to person, extends microphone.

Person (*stands, speaks*): Are you suggesting there is something wrong with buying an RV and a boat?

Dale (*shakes head*): No, that's not the point. The question is, which is more important in my life: *things*, or *people*? Do I satisfy my own personal greed before considering the need of anyone else? Or, do I make room in my budget for sharing God's blessings with others? My life was an exact replay of the parable of the rich young man in the book of Mark. (*Jabs thumb to his chest*): I was that rich man—I had more love for my money than for those around me. And my love of money was separating me from the love of God. (*Person sits down.*) Today, I find it hard to believe that we could have been so self-centered. We even celebrated those failed tax levies with our friends! By our standards, the results were a complete success: we saved money, invested it for a substantial gain, and had more money to spend on ourselves—exactly what we had planned. We completely failed to see the other results: the terrible impact of our decisions upon many helpless people, including that precious little girl.

Gerald: Once you recognized your mistake, what did you do?

Dale: That was the most humbling time of our lives! We spent a lot of time in prayer asking God's forgiveness for our terrible greed. Then we stepped out in faith.

Gerald: Would you describe what steps you took?

Dale: First, we found a couple who would take the little girl when she left the hospital. Then we organized a group to assist the most helpless victims of poverty—children.

Gerald: That's beautiful, Dale. Is that program still in operation?

Dale (*nods*): It certainly is, and on a much broader scale. Several city churches have combined their efforts in a united program to make sure nobody is refused help.

Gerald: Were there any other spin-offs from your decision that New Year's Day?

Dale: Together with *many* other families, we organized a camp that is still in operation. Thousands of young people from a three-county area have received many blessings from their week-long experiences at camp.

Gerald: Have these outreach programs had an impact upon your church budget?

Dale (*excitedly*): Not only the budget, but the growth of the church as well! The entire congregation became involved—many went from total apathy to enthusiastic support! Our membership doubled within two years and we've been able to extend our outreach to meet a variety of needs: home care for the disabled and elderly, and child care programs, as well as help for the homeless.

Gerald: There is another key player in this unforgettable scenario. (*Motions for Helen to come forward.*) This is Helen Brown, Dale's wife. (*Helen joins the group, shakes hands with Lisa and sits down.*)

Gerald (*to Helen*): Are there any other facts you wish to add?

Helen (*to Lisa*): I want to personally thank you for saving Dale's life. I was watching the program on a monitor backstage, and I got goose bumps when you told how you had taken a thirty-mile detour to go by the river. That had to be God's hand on your heart. Otherwise, Dale would have drowned.

Gerald (*to audience*): The question presented at the beginning of this program was, what compelled these two people to risk their lives so that total strangers might live? The answer appears to be, their decisions to accept and follow Jesus—to be His servants and stewards of His gifts. They presented their lives as living sacrifices in the face of personal disaster. And as a result of their Christian convictions, both that boy and Dale are alive today.

(*To Lisa, Dale and Helen*): Do any of you wish to give some advice to our audience regarding times when they are faced with difficult decisions?

Lisa: Each of us is bombarded daily with problems that require solutions. Some problems are simple, others are complex with dangerous consequences. The only way to make decisions with any degree of confidence is to rely on God's guidance.

Helen: We Christians have the option, indeed the duty, to act according to the teachings of Jesus—in other words, to be motivated always by love for others. Opportunities are all around us. What happened to that little girl twenty years ago could very well be happening in your community this very moment.

Dale: Jesus gives us a chance to start anew each day. Our separate journeys in faith begin *now*—this very minute—we can have "New Year's Day" every day of the year. As Paul wrote to the Christians in Rome, we must not let ourselves to be molded by society's standards.

Gerald (*to* Lisa, Dale *and* Helen, *with a broad smile on his face*): Before closing our program today, I would like to add one very important fact unknown to any of you. We just discovered this information last week.

(*Turns to audience*): As you have heard, twenty years ago Helen and Dale were deeply touched by a news story about a little girl found in a dumpster. As a direct result, they recommitted their lives to God and found a home for the little girl. They saved her from a life of poverty—and saved themselves from a life of selfish greed. The little girl was then adopted by a family who moved from this area. (*Pauses for a few seconds, then*): That small girl found in the alley (*points excitedly to* Lisa) was Lisa! (Lisa, Helen *and* Dale *sit wide-eyed in shock.*)

Lisa (*throws up her arms*): Praise the Lord! (*Leaps up, dashes to* Helen *and* Dale, *frantically embraces and kisses them.*)

CURTAIN

The Scourge of Scars

CHARACTERS

Michele Kern; wife, mother, loving, sensitive, feelings easily hurt, age 30-45
Jim Kern; Michele's husband, loving, sensitive, feelings easily hurt, age 30-45
Eric Kern; son of Michele and Jim, age 12, normal youth
Nancy Olson; Christian friend, patient, loving, age 30-45
Dave Olson; Christian friend, patient, caring, age 30-45
Mr. Caldwell; grade school principal, voice only

SCENES

Scene 1: Living room of Michele's apartment
Scene 2: Living room of Jim's apartment
Scene 3: Michele's apartment
Scene 4: Michele's apartment

PERFORMANCE TIPS

This play is performed on a stage split between two settings; Michele's apartment and Jim's apartment. You can furnish the two settings as elaborately or as simply as you wish beyond the props listed. Use a room divider to separate the apartments. The "door" to both apartments is stage front; character inside walks forward to an imaginary door.

Turn lights on and off to signal scene changes.

Voices on telephone may be prerecorded or performed live, offstage

PROPS

Cassette with taped sound effects and voices (if you choose not to do them live)

Two chairs, two Bibles, mail, magazines, letters
Photos, or cards representing photos
Two telephones, ball glove and cap
Dollar bills and a greeting card
Watch, and box for watch
End table or coffee table
Room divider

SCENE ONE *opens on Michele's apartment. She is reading her mail.*

Michele (*talks angrily to herself*): I hate to see the mail arrive! (*Holds up envelopes.*) Nothing but bills! (*Opens one, scans briefly, reads aloud*): "This is your fourth and final warning. If the full account balance is not paid within two weeks, we shall be forced to repossess your automobile!" (*Angrily throws it on floor.*) There's no way I can pay it! No job, and no money coming in! It's all Jim's fault! He knocks me down, then moves thirty miles away! For all he cares, Eric and I could starve to death! Why is he doing this to us? I even had to break our lease on Maple Avenue and move across town! (*Looks through a few more envelopes.*) There's no way I can pay these bills! (*Throws them to floor. Looks at last envelope.*) Here's something from Eric's new school. (*Puzzled, quickly opens it and reads*): "We are deeply concerned about Eric. He shows no interest in learning, fails to respond to questions, and avoids all efforts to make friends in his new school here at Adams Elementary." (*Looks up, angry.*) That's terrible! And all because of his father!

Eric (*enters room, long face*): Mom, I miss my friends at my old school. Can we move back to Maple Avenue?

Michele (*shakes head*): We can't afford it, Eric. We were lucky we were able to get this apartment through the welfare agency.

Eric (*head bowed*): I sure miss Kevin. He was my best friend.

Michele (*anger rising*): Your dad's to blame for *all* our problems! He hasn't sent a penny for support! He hasn't even called for over four months now!

Eric (*head in hands, sobs*): You're always blaming Dad. I don't even want to think about it. I'm going to bed. (*Leaves.*)

Michele (*shakes head angrily, looks up.*) What can I do to make him understand that Jim caused this mess? I *hate* that man!

Recorded sound *of knock on door.*

Michele (*opens door*): Oh! Hi, Nancy! It's nice to see you again! Come on in. Have a chair. (*Points to chair.*) I've missed seeing you and Dave. (*Both sit down.*)

Nancy (*nods*): Yes, it's been a long time. You didn't tell anyone where you were going! Dave and I have been trying to find you ever since you and Eric moved. Finally, I called all the schools until I got Eric's address.

Michele: Sorry. I've just been such a mess since Jim walked out on us four months ago.

Nancy: I know it must be terrible. How is Eric handling all this?

Michele: It's affecting him very badly—his grades at school, his attitude, even his health. I'm so worried about him.

Nancy: Kevin misses Eric terribly. He was really broken up when his closest buddy moved away.

Michele (*angrily*): Jim's to blame for everything! This whole mess started last year when his hours at the plant were cut in half. First, he started drinking! Then we started arguing constantly, and finally, he started chasing other women! Now he's forgotten we ever existed!

Nancy (*shakes head*): I'm so sorry to hear that.

Michele (*points to chin*): See that scar? Jim did that! The same night he walked out on us! I'll never forget it! Let me tell you what happened.

Lights go off and Nancy exits. Michele throws on a sweater and sits down with a magazine. Lights come up.

Jim (*staggers drunkenly in*): I thought you'd be in bed by now.

Michele (*angry*): You just *hoped* I'd be in bed! That way I wouldn't know what time you got home! (*Checks watch*): It's three in the morning! What *girl* were you out with tonight?

Jim (*glares at her*): You're *always* accusing me of running around! But you're dead wrong! Just because I had a couple of beers doesn't mean I've been chasing skirts!

Michele: That's a lie! It's no wonder we can't pay our bills! You spend it all on booze and women! (*Pushes him in chest. He staggers backward.*)

Jim (*angrily pushes her shoulder*): You've turned into a nagging witch! Don't blame me for your troubles!

Michele (*picks up magazines*): You're nothing but a drunken bum! (*Throws stack of magazines at him.*)

Jim: You can't get away with that! (*Hits her with back of hand.*)

Michele (*screams, falls to floor. She covers her chin with one hand, jabs her other finger in his direction*): So help me, someday I'll *kill* you! Now *get* out and *stay* out! And I hope I never see your *drunken* face again as *long* as I live!

Jim turns with fists clenched and stomps from room. Lights go off. Nancy returns as Michele removes sweater. They return to original positions. Lights come back on.

Michele (*angrily*): That's exactly how it happened! And on Valentine's Day at that!

Nancy: That was awful! I had no idea what you were suffering.

Michele (*points to scar*): His ring cut my chin and left this scar! I'll *never* forgive him as long as I live! Then after he left, Eric and I ran completely out of food! I couldn't even keep up the rent payments! That's when I had to turn to welfare to get this apartment. If Jim had his way, we'd have starved to death! The court ordered him to pay temporary support during our divorce proceedings, but he hasn't paid a penny!

Nancy: What can Dave and I do to help?

Michele (*shakes head*): It's degrading enough to be on welfare; I don't want to start asking my friends for money! We'll manage somehow. I just hope I can find a job soon.

Nancy: Our Sunday-school class is willing to help you. Why don't you come back this Sunday? You need all the help you can get—and we *all* need God's help!

Michele (*shakes head*): I'm too embarrassed to face them.

Nancy: But Michele, we named the class, "Sisters and Brothers" so that we'd remember to treat each other as members of the family of Christ. We want to be ready to help—whatever the problem.

Michele (*nods*): I understand that. But I'm just not ready yet.

Nancy (*sighs*): Michele, I've had several friends whose marriages have really been helped by a trained Christian counselor. Even if only one partner goes, that's a start toward finding solutions. What do you think?

Michele (*hesitates*): No, I couldn't handle that.

Nancy: Well, how about you and Eric coming over to visit? He and Kevin need each other badly.

Michele (*hesitates*): I'll think it over.

Nancy (*stands*): We'll keep you and Eric on our prayer list.

Michele: Thanks, Nancy. I appreciate that.

Nancy leaves, Michele picks up magazine, returns to chair.

End of Scene One

Scene Two: *Lights come up on Jim's apartment as he scans a magazine for a few seconds.*

Recorded sound *of telephone ringing.*

Jim: Hello, Jim Kern speaking.

Recorded voice: Mr. Kern, I'm Mr. Caldwell, principal at Adams Elementary. I received your note about Eric and am glad to hear that you're concerned. We're greatly concerned about him, too. His teacher has noticed his lack of interest in learning and complete lack of response. He also appears to be disinterested in making friends in his new school. Is there any way you can help him?

Jim (*angrily*): What a terrible thing for Eric! His mother is directly responsible! Since she refuses to let me even visit with him, my hands are tied! She acts like she doesn't care what happens to him!

Recorded voice: I'm sorry to hear that. We've done about all we can do to help him.

Jim: I just wish there were something I could do to help. But I can't even see him to talk to him.

Recorded voice: Let me know if you have any ideas. We'll work with you any way we can, for Eric's sake.

Jim (*hangs up, bewildered*): Can't she see what she's doing? Or does she even care? Oh Lord! Where can I turn for help?

Recorded sound *of knock on door.*

Jim (*walks over, opens door*): Hi, Dave. Come on in. (*Shakes hand.*) Haven't seen you in a long time.

Dave: Well, Nancy and I didn't know where to find you until yesterday. (*Both sit in chairs.*) We've missed seeing you in church and Sunday school.

Jim: Sorry about that. My whole world has fallen apart. But I didn't want to cause anybody to worry, so I decided to drop out for a while.

Dave: But that's what our "Sisters and Brothers" class is all about—helping each other in times of trouble. And you've certainly had some *real* troubles.

Jim (*nods*): My life has gone from bad to worse ever since my hours at the plant were cut in half. Michele acted like she never understood what that meant. She just kept on buying things like she always did.

Dave: It must be tough trying to live on half your income.

Jim: I can't count the times I told her, "Can't you understand at all? We just can't spend more than I bring home!" She never got the message. (*Points thumb downward*): So down we went—close to bankruptcy. It was driving me crazy!

Dave (*nods head*): That was a real bad time for you.

Jim: That's when we dropped out of church. We just couldn't face our friends. And I couldn't stand her vicious nagging and screaming! So I started hitting the bars. I really had no other choice. She even accused me of chasing women. Then on Valentine's Day, I bought her a card to try to make up to her. But when I got home, she started shoving me around and threw a stack of magazines at me. So I let her have it—right across the mouth! I can't say I'm sorry. She deserved it!

Dave: Was she hurt?

Jim (*shrugs shoulders*): I don't know. She ordered me to get out and stay out. (*Angrily*): She even threatened to *kill* me! Two days later I was arrested for domestic violence. Before it was all over, I had spent three days in jail. (*Angrily*): And after that, I lost my job! (*Slaps hand to knee.*) Just *try* to get a decent job with a criminal record! (*Lowers head.*) I can't fully describe how it feels to be unemployed—totally helpless and useless. (*Gestures angrily with hands*): And now I can't even pay the support the judge ordered! (*Wipes his eyes.*)

Dave: Do you have any prospects for getting a job?

Jim (*nods*): *Finally*—after all this time—with the sanitation department. It starts next week. I hate it, but it's a job.

Dave: How have you managed to survive?

Jim: I'm ashamed to admit it, but my parents have paid all my bills, including the rent on this apartment. I hate being dependent upon anyone. (*Angrily*): And it's *all* her fault!

Dave: I'm glad you finally found work, even though it's not what you're trained for. At least it's a start. (*Pause*.) Jim, how about coming to class this Sunday? Maybe you'd hear something that could be of help to you—and wouldn't you like to see your friends again?

Jim (*hesitates*): Well, maybe after I start my new job.

Dave: Would you consider talking to Michele about visiting with Eric? He needs you badly. You and he have always been best buddies.

Jim (*angrily shakes head*): Every time I tried to see Eric, Michele started in again—arguing and screaming! *Right* in front of him! That last visit was a total disaster! I took a couple of drinks at a bar to work up the courage to face her. I'll never forget what happened as long as I live!

Lights switch to Michele's apartment. Dave remains motionless in Jim's apartment throughout the flashback. Jim throws on a jacket, walks to front of stage on Michele's side, pretends to knock on door.

Recorded sound *of knock on door.*

Michele *walks over, opens door.*

Jim (*rudely*): I'm here to get Eric.

Michele (*leans forward and sniffs*): You've been drinking again!

Jim: Like I said, I'm here to get Eric.

Michele (*nastily*): When are you *ever* going to stop drinking and *start* paying support?

Jim (*equally nasty*): When I get a job, *you'll* get your money!

Michele: But the judge ordered you to start paying two months ago! (*Holds out hand, grins*): So pay up!

Jim (*starts to slap her hand, she pulls it back*): I told you *you'll* get your money when I get a job! Is Eric ready to go?

Michele (*taunting*): How do I know I can trust you with Eric? You just might slap him around like you did me!

Jim (*clenches fist at side, yells*): Bring Eric to the door—right now!

Michele: You never did listen to anything I said!

Jim (*yells*): And I don't have to listen to your loud mouth now! The judge gave me the right to visit Eric!

Michele (*screams*): He also said, "*pay support*!" You'll see Eric when you start paying, and not until then!

Jim *angrily turns to leave.*

Michele (*screams*): You're nothing but a *drunken* bum! I don't *ever* want to see you again! You *hear*? *Ever*!

Lights off. Jim quickly removes his jacket and returns to chair on his side. Lights come up on his side.

Jim: That's exactly how it happened, Dave, and as I left, I noticed Eric looking out the window, crying his heart out. (*Bows head, wipes eyes.*) He heard the whole thing—he's *caught* right in the middle! (*Angrily*): She doesn't even care *what* happens to him!

Dave: That was terrible. I feel so sorry for Eric. Has he ever gotten to see your parents since you and Michele separated?

Jim: Just one time! That's it! After my last attempt to visit, Mom called Michele about stopping by to see Eric. They hadn't seen him in over four months. When she agreed, they stopped by. Eric was *really* excited. Then Mom asked him, "Has your scout leader planned a camp-out soon? Your dad asked me to find out." That's when Michele glared at her and snapped, "Don't you *ever* mention him around here again!" They were shocked, and deeply hurt. So they gave Eric a hug and left. (*Slams fist to leg.*) *Right* in front of Eric! Now we're all cut off from seeing him!

Dave (*shakes head*): That must have been terrible for Eric.

Jim: I was so mad, I called my attorney and told him to sue for custody! *That'll* teach her a lesson!

Dave: Jim, when people have such severe problems as you have, they desperately need help. Why don't you come back to church?

Jim: Thirty miles is just too far to drive.

Dave: How about talking with a Christian counselor?

Jim (*angrily*): I don't need help! *She's* the one who needs help!

Dave: I'm sorry you feel that way, Jim. We'll keep you on our prayer list. (*They stand, shake hands.*)

Jim: Thanks, Dave. I certainly appreciate that.

Dave leaves, Jim sits down in chair.

END OF SCENE TWO

SCENE THREE: *Lights come up on Michele's apartment.*

Michele (*takes letter from envelope*): A letter from Nancy! She never quits trying to help—I hear from her at least once a week. (*Opens envelope, scans letter.*)

Nancy's recorded voice: Dear Michele: I thought I'd drop you a note to bring you up-to-date. We missed Eric at the church youth picnic. Kevin was looking forward to seeing him again. The other day, Dave and I were looking through an old photo album and came across many pictures of our two families. We thought you and Eric might enjoy looking at them, so I'm sending them along. They brought back many wonderful memories of our boys growing up. I also thought of something else that might help you: 1 Corinthians 13, the love chapter. The message is a tough one, but vitally important for everyone. When reading that chapter, I was reminded again that love requires spiritual help to maintain. Best wishes to both of you. We love you, and God loves you. Nancy.

Michele looks at the photos. The dialogue may be typed on pieces of paper the size and shape of photographs.

Michele: Isn't that beautiful—Eric, just one month old. (*Looks up.*) The miracle of birth, and tiny legs and arms, and fingers that move and grip. Thank you, God. (*Next photo.*) Eric and Kevin in the city park. Let's see, they'd be close to five then. (*Next one.*) Eric's sixth birthday—at our house. There's Jim hugging him. That's touching. I'd forgotten about that. (*Next one.*) Eric's first ball game in the church youth league. (*Points excitedly*): There's Eric at first base. And Kevin's playing shortstop. (*Looks up, reflecting*): They must have been about eleven at that time. (*Back to photo.*) And there's Dave and Jim on the sidelines. They certainly enjoyed those games. And so did Eric and Kevin. (*Next photo.*) Both of our families at the state fair. (*Happily*): The Blue Devil ride with Eric waving down at us. I can still hear them laughing and screaming. (*Lays down photos, reaches for* Bible.) I'll look up that love chapter. (*Turns to it, moves finger down page.*) Here it is. (*Reads to self, looks up.*) It talks about patience, kindness and forgiveness. It says that love doesn't demand its own way. (*Closes* Bible, *puzzled. Silent for two seconds, then shakes her head.*)

Recorded sound *of telephone ringing.*

Michele: Kern residence. Michele speaking.

Nancy's recorded voice: Hi, Michele. This is Nancy. I thought I'd give you a call to see how you're coming along.

Michele: Okay, I guess.

Nancy: Have you received my note yet?

Michele: Yes, and I appreciated it very much. I particularly enjoyed the photographs. They brought back a lot of beautiful memories. I'd forgotten all those fun times our two families enjoyed together.

Nancy: We certainly have had our share of them—more than many families have in a lifetime. (*Pause*): Those Bible verses I mentioned have meant a lot to me over the years. Did you get a chance to look at them?

Michele: Yes, I did. I realize their importance. But I don't think you understand just how difficult it is for me to think about forgiveness—or love—at this time.

Nancy: Perhaps I do understand. Some scars seem to be branded on one's heart forever. But they don't have to continue hurting. Since scars are beyond our human capacity to remove, we need God's help and a strong faith to heal them.

Michele (*hesitates*): I guess you're right. It's just that . . . well, everything's so difficult. I don't know where to turn, or where to start. Right now, forgiving Jim is extremely tough.

Nancy: When I struggle with forgiving someone, I try to think of Jesus on the cross. He forgave those soldiers who had scourged Him, nailed Him to the cross, and were ridiculing His divinity! That was many times more difficult than any problem we'll *ever* face in our entire lives. And He allowed all of that to be done to Him because of *our* sins—because He loved us enough to want us to be forgiven! Michele, when I think of that, my reasons for holding a grudge against someone usually seem kind of petty.

Michele (*hesitates*): Well, it's certainly worth some serious thought.

Nancy: There's something else that's worth some serious thought, Michele. God's Word teaches us that we will be forgiven *as we forgive others*. You and Jim are both Christians—you're going to have to come to the place where you can forgive each other—wouldn't it be better to try to save your marriage?

Michele (*sighs*): I'm sure you're right. At times I miss Jim terribly. It's a back-and-forth thing. I don't know—how can I be sure he won't hurt me again?

Nancy (*laughs kindly*): I'm sure you can be sure that he *will* hurt you again—and you will hurt him. Neither one of you is perfect! But that's where commitment comes in—and trusting in God to see you through whatever happens.

Michele (*hesitates*): Well, I'll think it over.

Nancy: In the meantime, maybe we can help Eric through all this. The church youth team has a game next Saturday. If you could bring him to church Sunday, he'd be eligible to play in the game the following weekend. What do you think?

Michele: I'll do it. And I'll plan on staying for the game.

Nancy: Wonderful! We'll see you in class Sunday.

Michele (*hangs up.*) Eric will love it! (*Places Bible into end table drawer.*) Oh, there's Jim's watch. (*Holds it up, smiles.*) I remember the night he received it—at his company's annual banquet. (*Looks up.*) That was back when we were still dating. (*Looks back at watch.*) It was a very special award. (*Reads from back of watch*): "James Kern—Employee of the Year." (*Looks up.*) I was so proud of him. (*Hesitates, then shakes head.*) And then, just thirteen years later, we had that bad fight. When he slapped me, his watch flew off and smashed against the floor (*looks at watch*), shattering the crystal. That's when I decided to save it. That way I'd never forget what he did to me. (*Hesitates, looks upward.*) Can I *really* forgive him? Like Jesus did those soldiers—and like God forgives me? (*Hand to forehead.*) It'll take some effort—and some faith!

And those photos. . . I had forgotten just how loving a man Jim can be. (*Bows head.*) Lord, give me the courage and the faith to forgive him. He means so much to Eric and to me. I didn't realize just how important he was until this very moment. Please erase the memory of this scar on my chin. And the deeper scars in my heart. They've been slowly choking the very life out of me. (*Looks up, puzzled.*) What did Nancy say? Neither one of us is perfect. . . . She's absolutely right! (*Drops head.*) I've treated Jim terribly over the years. . . . Oh Lord, please forgive me!

Light goes down on her side, up on Jim's side.

Jim (*holds up envelope*): A letter from Dave! (*Eagerly opens and removes letter. Reads it carefully.*)

Dave's recorded voice: Dear Jim: Since we haven't talked for over a week now, I thought I'd write you a note. I hope everything's okay on your new job.

Eric wasn't able to attend the church youth picnic last week, and Kevin was really disappointed. He had been looking forward to seeing his old buddy again.

The other day, Nancy and I stumbled across our old photo album. It showed many pictures of our two families doing things together. I've enclosed copies of a few pictures you might enjoy.

I also thought of several Bible verses that might help you: 1 Corinthians 13—the love chapter. I've learned one, very important lesson from those verses, in any argument, it doesn't matter who is right and who is wrong. The only thing that *really* matters is that I listen, respond, and act in love at all times. Although I don't always live up to it, I give it my best shot—with God's help.

I'll try to call you in a few days to see how you're getting along. Dave.

Jim (*lays down letter, looks up*): That Dave really hangs in there. He either calls or writes once a week. That's Christian love in action. (*Looks at photos.*) There's Eric when he was just a few weeks old! He added a new dimension to our lives—made a three-way love affair. (*Pauses, sighs.*) I'm still deeply touched by God's miracle of birth. (*Next picture.*) There's my buddy—in the city park. He certainly was a happy boy. (*Next one.*) Eric's sixth birthday, hugging his old dad. That's the same year he started to school. (*Next one.*) There he is at first base. He certainly loves playing softball. Jim and I never missed a single game over all those years. (*Next one.*) The state fair—all six of us. And the Blue Devil ride! With Eric screaming at us! (*Lays photos down.*) What wonderful memories. (*Looks up.*) Lord, what can I do to help make *new* memories, just like those earlier ones? (*Opens Bible.*) I'll look at that love chapter. (*Finds it.*) Here it is. (*Reads to himself silently for a few seconds.*) It says, be patient, kind and forgiving. And do not be jealous, selfish, or rude. (*Looks up.*) When we had that fight on Valentine's Day, I can't believe I slapped her so hard, my watch fell off. That's rudeness in its worst form. (*Hand to head.*) And back when I took those marriage vows, I promised God to love and cherish her forever. (*Bows head.*) Please Lord, help me. I need forgiveness in the worst way. Give me the courage to step out in faith. (*Looks up, puzzled.*) But what if she won't change?

Recorded sound *of telephone ringing.*

Jim: Jim Kern speaking.

Dave's recorded voice: Hi Jim, Dave here. How's your new job coming along?

Jim: Glad you called. It's working out better than I expected.

Dave: That's good news, Jim. (*Excitedly*): I can't wait to tell you about Eric! Michele decided to come back to church and that made Eric eligible for the church youth softball team. Last Saturday, he got to play, and he hit the game-winning home run!

Jim (*excited, happy*): That's great!

Dave: Jim, Eric is really enjoying his friends again. Being with them has *really* changed him, he's like a new boy!

Jim (*speaks with great difficulty*): I'm so choked up, I can hardly talk.

Dave: I've got an idea. Why don't you call Michele and ask to take her and Eric to the game tomorrow?

Jim (*hesitates*): I'm afraid she'll make a scene.

Dave: Maybe not. Nancy tells me that she's changed quite a bit in the past two weeks.

Jim: Well, I could give it a try. Do you have her new number?

Dave: Sure do: 348-6509. I'll hang up so you can call her.

Lights come up on both sides. Michele is sitting in a chair reading a magazine. Jim shakes his head, unsure, stands and walks around the room for a few seconds. Then he bows his head for a few seconds, gestures as if making a decision, and quickly returns to chair and dials telephone.

Recorded sound *of telephone ringing.*

Michele (*picks up telephone*): Hello, Michele Kern speaking.

Jim (*hesitant, awkward*): Hi. This is Jim. I thought I'd give you a call to see how you were doing.

Michele (*hesitant, awkward*): I'm fine, thanks. Ah . . . how are you doing?

Jim: Fine here, too. (*Long silence.*) I . . . I just heard from Dave. He told me about you and Eric going back to church. I was glad to hear that.

Michele (*hesitant*): Yeah. I really enjoyed seeing our church friends again. I also got to talk with Nancy and Dave a little bit.

Jim: Glad to hear that. Dave mentioned how much Eric has changed.

Michele: Yes, he certainly has. He's really happy to get back with his many friends at church.

Jim: That's wonderful. (*Pause.*) I don't know how to say this. I . . . I feel awkward asking you this. How about me stopping by tomorrow and taking you and Eric to the game?

Michele (*hesitates*): Well, I . . . I guess that sounds okay.

Jim (*surprised*): Really? Uh, okay! I'll see you around two.

Both hang up. Lights go off.

End of Scene Three

Scene Four: *Lights come up on Michele's apartment to reveal her humming excitedly as she straightens up the room. Eric enters wearing a baseball cap and carrying a ball glove.*

Eric (*excitedly*): I can't wait for Dad to get here! I've been praying for this day for over six months now!

Michele: He told me yesterday how happy he was to learn how things are going for you. And I feel the same way. During the past few months, I've let my selfish pride overpower my love for you. Please forgive me, Eric.

Eric: I'll love you no matter what happens. (*Hugs her.*) And Dad, too. I never felt any happier in my life. (*Excitedly*): Do you have his watch ready for him?

Michele: It's all set. I picked it up this morning—the new crystal looks great!. Oh! I forgot to get a card to put with it! (*Get purse, hands* Eric *a couple of dollar bills.*) Would you run over to the store and buy an appropriate card—something like, "We love you," or, "We've missed you"?

Eric (*takes money*): Sure! I'll be right back. (*Exits.*)

Michele (*looks at watch*): I can't wait to see Jim's reaction!

She places the watch in a box, then puts the box in the table drawer. Jim approaches, knocks on door. At first, their conversation is hesitant, very awkward, with short silences.

Michele (*opens door*): Hi, Jim. Come on in.

Jim (*nervously*): Hi, Michele.

Michele (*points*): Have a seat. (*Both walk to chairs in silence.*)

Jim: Ah . . . . nice day today, isn't it?

Michele: Yes, it is.

Jim: Much better than yesterday.

Michele (*nods*): I was afraid it might rain and they'd cancel the game. But so far, we're in luck.

Jim (*looks around*): Is Eric around?

Michele: He's running an errand. He should be back soon.

Jim: I was delighted to hear how things are going for him.

Michele: He has *really* changed. I've never seen him any happier. And he's especially excited about seeing you again.

Jim: I feel the same about both of you. (*Pause.*) This is probably the most important day for me in many years.

Michele (*nods*): Jim, I've been trying to work up the courage to tell you something. It's . . . it's hard to find the right words to say. I want to apologize to you for everything I've said and done to you. I don't know what got into me. You were right—I was acting like a witch. I couldn't see it then, but I do now.

Jim (*deeply touched*): Those are the most precious words I've ever heard. (*Wipes eyes.*) I never thought I could *ever* be forgiven for slapping you—on Valentine's Day of all times. It's the worst thing I've ever done, much worse than those other things I've said and done to you.

Michele: You're forgiven. The slate's been wiped clean.

Jim (*goes to her side, she stands, they hold hands*): And yours, too. My prayers have been answered. I can't thank Dave enough for his dedication and support over the past six months.

Michele: The same for Nancy. Her love never gave up—just like in I Corinthians 13. (*They fall into an embrace and kiss.*)

Eric (*tosses card on table or couch, runs to Jim excitedly*): Hi, Dad! It's so good to see you again! (*Hugs him.*)

Jim: It's really great to see you, too, Eric! You're looking good! I was glad to hear you're back with your church friends, particularly Kevin.

Eric: It sure is fun being with them again!

Jim (*gently pushes Eric's shoulder*): And how about that home run last Saturday! That was great!

Eric: Thanks, Dad. Let me show you something. (*Dashes to end table, returns with paper, hands to Jim*): This is the church newsletter. (*Points to letter*): Look on page two!

Jim (*opens, reads aloud*): "We were happy to see Michele and Eric Kern back with us last Sunday. Their class friends were especially delighted to see them again. And Eric, congratulations on that winning home run." (*Looks up excitedly*): How about that? They certainly were happy to see both of you. (*Looks at each in turn*): And I'm even *more* happy to see you both again.

Eric goes to end table drawer, picks up box with watch, picks up card, holds both behind him as he returns to Jim.

Eric (*hands card and box to Jim*): Here, Dad! We've got a surprise for you!

Jim (*reads card aloud. Then*): That's wonderful! (*Looks to each.*) I love both of you very much, too. (*Opens box, looks shocked, then slowly holds watch up*): Isn't that simply beautiful!

Eric: You must have been a real good worker to get a special award like that! It says "Employee of the Year," on the back!

Jim: Thanks, Eric. This watch symbolizes an unforgettable night in my life, one I'll treasure forever.

Michele: I was so proud of you when you received it!

Jim: To me it represents an event even greater than the award; that was the same night I proposed to you. And you accepted!

Michele: That's right! The same night! I knew the watch was important to you, but I didn't know you remembered that was the night you proposed!

Jim: To me, it was always a reminder of our love. And still is.

Michele: Jim, I. . . I'm kinda choked up here! (*They both laugh a little.*) This morning, I was thinking about the day we decided to tie the knot. I got so mushy, I called my lawyer and dropped the divorce.

Jim: Oh, Michele, I'm so glad to hear that! (*Reaches into his pocket and pulls out card, excitedly*): This is for you. (*Hands her card.*) It's a valentine. (*She looks at him oddly.*) I've had it for six months. I was going to give it to you the night we had that big fight. I was hoping *then* we could make up and quit arguing and fighting.

Michele (*stunned, opens and reads card silently. Then*): Oh, Jim, that's beautiful! I had no idea you had planned to make up! (*Hugs him tightly, kisses him. Then she leans back and looks into his eyes*): Why don't you come back home to stay—forever? Then we can celebrate Valentine's Day all year long.

Jim: I've hoped and prayed you'd ask me that, honey. Just in case you did, I packed my suitcase and brought it along!

All three laugh happily and fall into an embrace.

CURTAIN

The Greatest Power

Characters
Mr. Bismark; Director of the Department of Religious Obedience, overbearing, bossy, age 50-60
Ruth Nelson; Assistant, practical businesswoman, age 25-40
Keith Garrison; Department detective, tough, age 25-40
Governor Kaiser; Businessman, answers to Bismark, well dressed, calm, well organized, age 50-60
TV News Anchor; well dressed, age 30-40
Becky Fordham; Lottery winner, calm, warm hearted, age 25-40
Four Voices; recorded for playback, or performed live

Scenes
Scene 1: Office of Deptartment of Religious Obedience
Scene 2: Same office several days later

Performance Tips

Play is performed on a split stage. One side is the office of the federal "Department of Religious Obedience," (so identified with a sign) and the other side is a large TV

The office setting has a conference table, four chairs, a two-way radio (or facsimile, or telephone), and five sets of papers. Options for the TV setting include using a real TV set with prerecorded programs, or a large TV "frame," within which your characters will act. If the stage represents the TV set, display a sign, "CHANNEL 8 TV."

To provide more impact, use names of local places wherever indicated.

Use lights to signal scene changes.

For the "voice from Heaven," use two or more speakers along the sides of the of stage with a loud booming voice. Actors/actresses will, of course, be as shocked as the audience is!

Props

Office chairs, table, and sign: DEPARTMENT OF RELIGIOUS OBEDIENCE

Cassette with prerecorded sound effects and voices
Two-way radio, or facsimile, or telephone
TV set, remote control, drinking glasses
Stereo speakers, for "the voice of God"
Five sets of folders, papers
Pistol and holster

Scene One: *Lights come up on an empty office. Ruth and Keith enter, happy and excited, and take the two middle seats at the table. Ruth is carrying a computer printout and a folder with papers, Keith is wearing a holster and pistol and is carrying a folder with papers.*

Ruth: You did it, Keith! You finally got enough evidence to arrest that man, Jesus! This is the biggest crime bust in U. S. history!

Keith (*smiles*): Our dedicated team of investigators went all the way to crack this case! We used every known trick—bugs in his motel room, around-the-clock surveillance, and several under-cover spies.

Ruth: Fantastic job!

Keith: Thanks, Ruth. What really broke the case open was Julius Escarriot. He was one of Jesus' inner circle of twelve. When he called me at home that night (*chuckles*), I was shocked. He offered to tell us everything Jesus ever said and did. It cost us a bundle—$30,000—but the info we got was worth every penny.

Ruth (*smiles*): And now Jesus is on death row, awaiting execution!

Keith: When Director Bismark arrives, we'll give him enough solid evidence to convince Governor Kaiser to approve our recommendation to execute. (*Slaps hand to table.*)

Ruth: But what if the governor refuses? I've been concerned about his attitude ever since this Jesus began preaching. The Governor has shown absolutely no interest whatsoever in stopping this propaganda from being spread! I'm not sure we can trust him!

Keith: Not to worry. Although Bismark has no power to prevent Governor Kaiser's veto, he does have the authority to fire him anytime he wants.

Ruth: I sure hope you're right. This guy Jesus is about to destroy all we stand for—our national religion and our government. The law is clear: only one religion permitted—that of the National Temple. That's it! But this Jesus guy acts like he's above the law!

Keith (*shakes head*): No problem. He'll be executed tomorrow in (   ) Square/Park along with those two murderers.

Ruth: Then we can get our country back on the right track, both politically and economically.

Bismark (*enters angrily, walks quickly to table. Ruth and Keith stand until Bismark is seated.*) This man *must* be put to death! His bizarre ideas on religion are sweeping the country! He and his followers are about to cause a revolution among the people we've worked so hard to control! As director of the Federal Department of Religious Obedience (*shakes fist*), it's my responsibility to ensure that all citizens of the Imperial United States worship according to the directives of the National Temple! This Jesus is teaching direct disobedience! (*Slams fist on table.*) We've got to convince Governor Kaiser that this Jesus must be stopped—permanently!

Ruth: Is there any chance the governor will veto our department's decision to execute?

Bismark: He knows better. I've got him (*presses thumb to table, grins*) under my thumb! Either he approves it, or he's out on the street looking for a job. It's that simple! Captain Garrison, do you have any new information we can use when the governor gets here?

Keith: No, nothing new, just more of the same mutinous, anti-governmental propaganda. We learned from the bug on his phone that he planned to speak at the (hotel/lodge) along (street/freeway). So we were there, ready to tape his speech. (*Hands Bismark a set of stapled papers.*) Here's a transcript of it.

Bismark (*skims the pages, grows angrier*): Just listen to this crazy stuff! He's saying that those people who are persecuted because they follow God will be blessed and will go to Heaven! (*Looks up.*) How can anyone believe that being persecuted will bring them blessings?

Keith (*shakes head*): That's as bizarre as another theory he often talks about. He insists that love is, or has, some kind of power. And his followers believe it! (*Shakes head.*) That makes no sense at all.

Bismark: Ridiculous! What a wimp that guy is! Nobody in the history of the world has ever gotten to power, or retained their power, through love! The authority to rule a country comes only through maximum, brutal force—guns, rockets, and bombs!

Keith (*pats gun on hip*): That's the way it works!

Bismark: And that's the way it's going to stay!

Keith: All through our investigation, we've picked up two other words he's used again and again: "kingdom" and "power." He claims that when he is king, he'll be in power! That's revolutionary talk!

Bismark: We should have arrested him after he drove those flea market exhibitors out of the ( ) Street Temple. If only King Harold had done his job back when that star appeared above Bethlehem, we wouldn't have this problem today!

Keith: He even predicted his own death and told his close friends he'd be raised from the dead three days later! (*Angrily*): They're convinced he's speaking for God! That's when we arrested him!

Bismark: Did he put up any resistance?

Keith: No, but one of his accomplices cut off Sergeant Dunn's ear with a knife. And then Jesus touched Dunn's head as if to heal it. (*Puzzled*): And it worked! His ear was healed! (*Shakes head*): I don't understand that.

Bismark: It had to be faked. Just like those other so-called miracles you picked up in your investigation. Captain, you've done a fantastic job. You're in for a promotion after the firing squad performs its patriotic duty.

Keith (*smiles proudly*): Thanks, chief.

Bismark (*to Ruth*): We need to inform Governor Kaiser of the disastrous impact of Jesus' sermons on our national economy. What does the latest financial report show?

Ruth (*opens folder, pulls out printout*): This shows us in the red, with cash flow at its lowest point ever. We've been losing members and contributions since the first day he started preaching. As of last Monday, the National Temple enrollment has dropped half a million in just two years.

Bismark (*shocked*): That's a 10,000 dollar loss in one month!

Ruth (*nods*): It means we've had to cut back on staff, particularly at our casino and ski resorts across the country. Do you think we should put a hold on our plans for that new golf complex?

Bismark (*shakes head*): No way I'll let that happen! After our firing squad is finished, we'll be on our way up—back to normal. Have you heard from Erickson in the Division of Economics?

Ruth: She wasn't able to make the meeting today. She's working on that bank emergency. It's much worse than that depression back in the thirties—a direct result of Jesus' preaching. His followers are withdrawing their savings to help the poor. Several small S & L's have been forced to close, and three of them have already filed for bankruptcy.

Bismark: Do you have any statistics showing the trends?

Ruth (*pulls out printout, reads. To simplify this part, type the script onto the paper*): 1) Food service profits are off 15 percent. That was a direct result of Jesus feeding more than 10,000 people on Mount (   ) (*Or use name of local park.*) 2) Legal service revenues are down 23 percent due to a drastic reduction in crime and fewer lawsuits against what his followers call, "neighbors and brothers."

Bismark: That means cutbacks in our courts and law enforcement! There's no way I'll let that happen!

Ruth (*looks back at papers*): And our Medical services have experienced an 18 percent drop in revenues. This is due to his alleged, unverified healings across the country. (*Looks up*): Doctors report a huge drop in headaches, stomach troubles, ulcers, insomnia, tension therapy and counseling services. Jesus calls it "having peace in your heart," and "living in faith." If this trend continues, we're headed for the worst economic depression ever. (*Angrily*): He *must* be executed!

Keith: As soon as the governor okays it (*pats gun*), problem solved. We can execute tomorrow.

Bismark: And even if he doesn't approve it, the execution is still on!

Recorded sound: *of two-way radio or telephone ringing*

Keith (*answering the call*): Office of Religious Obedience, Captain Garrison speaking.

Recorded voice of O'Neil: Sergeant O'Neil reporting. I've been tailing one of Jesus' followers named Pete, also known as Rocky. We're at (   ) Restaurant where an interesting thing just happened. I heard three different customers ask him if he knew Jesus. And each time he answered, "No, I've never met him." (*Excitedly*): This guy is one of Jesus' closest allies and now appears to be deserting the team. It looks like Jesus is losing his followers!

Keith (*excitedly*): That's the best news I've heard all day!

Recorded O'Neil: And our informer, Escarriot, confirmed our suspicions about the words that are used in what they call, "The Lord's Prayer." It ends with, "For thine is the kingdom, the power, and the glory forever." There they are again, those same words: kingdom and power.

Keith: Right! Thanks for checking in! (*Hangs up.*) Hear that? Jesus is losing his support!

Bismark (*grins*): Now they're getting smart. With all this evidence, there's no way the governor can turn us down!

Kaiser *enters with folder, nods to each, sits at table.*

Bismark: Good afternoon, Governor. We need to discuss this man, Jesus. He's trying to take over our religion and government. (*Points to the governor's folder*): You have our reports. We're holding him in death row awaiting your decision.

Kaiser (*speaks slowly*): I've checked with the Attorney General, searching for legal grounds to execute. So far, we've come up empty-handed.

Bismark (*angrily*): That folder's filled with more than enough grounds! He's a revolutionary, trying to take over our temple and our government! And worst of all—*my* power!

Keith (*points to Kaiser's notes*): The reports are all in your folder! And every one has been confirmed by our inside snitch. The words that Jesus uses again and again are "kingdom" and "power"! To me, that calls for a firing squad!

Ruth: And his impact on our economy is a disaster. (*Reads from notes*): 1) Food service profits—down 15 percent; 2) Legal service revenues—down 23 percent; and 3) Medical service income—18 percent drop. That's enough evidence right there to execute him!

Kaiser (*speaks slowly and distinctly*): I've carefully studied all his speeches. I've picked up two consistent themes: loving your enemies, and forgiving others. Those are hardly what I'd call anti-government teachings!.

Bismark (*bitterly*): It's a cover-up! Can't you see? He's trying to replace our government with his kingdom!

Kaiser (*shakes head*): Even with all your evidence, I still see no capital crime.

Bismark: But just consider the results of his teaching going unchecked: economic disaster in banks, legal and medical services! And that means staff cuts in our department because there's not enough money to pay our salaries! And we may even lose our lives before *his* firing squad! Isn't that enough of a threat?

Kaiser: You still have nothing that requires the death penalty.

Bismark: Since he's talked about dying and coming back, why not execute him? Then when he fails to return, his cohorts will know he's been lying to them—that'll be the end of the revolution! (*Speaks slowly and distinctly with a broad grin*): I'll still be in charge, and you (*points finger toward the Governor*): won't lose your job!

Kaiser (*shocked*): What do you mean, "I won't lose my job"?

Bismark (*grins, jabs finger toward to Kaiser, speaks slowly and precisely*): If you don't approve the execution, Governor, we'll do it anyway! And you'll be fired—immediately! (*Grins.*) It's that simple!

Kaiser (*head down, studies paper*): I got your message. (*Pause.*) In that case, there's another way to resolve it. Our law permits us to release one death-row prisoner on our emperor's birthday—which is this weekend. Who shall we release: Jesus, or one of the murderers?

Bismark (*thinks for a second*): Release Doug Hawk.

Ruth (*angrily*): But he's the maniac who butchered his wife and two children!

Bismark: He's also my wife's cousin. Hawk gets released.

Kaiser (*shocked*): I can't believe it! You'd rather have a vicious murderer like Hawk loose on the streets than a peace preacher like Jesus?

Bismark (*angrily*): You got it! Hawk gets released!

Kaiser (*head bowed*): This case is now out of my hands. (*Glares at Bismark*): I hope you can live with your decision. (*Quickly closes his folder, stands and leaves.*)

Bismark (*claps hands*): Didn't I tell you? (*Grins.*) He knows where his paycheck comes from! (*To Keith*): He's all yours, Captain Garrison!

End of Scene One

Scene Two: *Lights come up on the office side of stage. Bismark, Ruth, and Keith stand sipping drinks—they are having a victory celebration. Ruth holds a remote control. Reporter and Becky are seated on* TV *side (beneath the* CHANNEL 8 TV *sign and behind* TV *frame.*

Bismark (*holds glass high*): Here's to the Department of Religious Obedience. The power of brutal force has saved our country from that traitor, Jesus!

Ruth and Keith (*raise glasses, shout*): Great! Yeah! (*Take a sip.*)

Ruth (*to Bismark*): I appreciate that 10 percent bonus you gave the department staff after the execution the other day.

Keith (*holds glass high*): I'll drink to that! And the firing squad members appreciated it, too! They did a fine job.

Bismark: Each of you deserved it—and more. You performed your patriotic duties perfectly. (*To Ruth*): That printed program you distributed for the execution holiday festivities was something else! Particularly that short history of Jesus' attempted takeover of the government.

Ruth (*nods*): Thanks, Chief.

Bismark: And that execution lottery you set up was a fantastic idea: selling chances to win Jesus' watch and billfold really brought in the money!

Ruth (*nods, smiles*): And the dance in (   ) Park came off perfectly. (*To Keith*): Your fireworks display provided the perfect finale for the celebration.

Keith: Thanks, Ruth. I saved that idea for the most important execution in U. S. history.

Bismark: I just received a call from Channel 8. They'll be reporting on several events relating to the Jesus matter on the six-o'clock news. One part will include an interview with the woman who won the execution lottery.

Ruth: Sounds great. She must be the happiest person alive.

Bismark: Channel 8 had a tough time finding her for the interview today. She disappeared shortly after the execution.

Keith: That's strange. After winning the lottery, I expected to see her name in the headlines, or see her on some talk show by now.

Bismark (*to Keith*): While we're waiting, I want to announce your promotion to Second Assistant in the Department of Religious Obedience. Congratulations! (*Shakes Keith's hand.*)

Keith: Thanks, Chief. If Jesus' revolutionary speeches had continued, our department would have been forced to shut down. And we'd all be out of jobs. Escarriot made the difference. He deserves a medal for his deep patriotism. By the way, has anyone heard anything about him since the night of the execution?

Ruth (*excitedly*): Oh! I forgot to tell you! I was checking some last-minute details with the receptionist at the main desk the night of the execution when he dashed in and practically *threw* that bag of money at us—all $30,000! Then he rushed back out without a comment. (*Hesitates*): The only thing I could figure was that someone was after him and he wanted to stash the money someplace safe—I'm holding it for him.

Bismark (*puzzled*): I saw something a little strange, too. Channel 8 interviewed some of his neighbors to get the "home town hero angle," but they reported that instead of being excited, he was upset. He left the neighborhood shortly before the execution and so far, hasn't returned. I've listened to all the news reports since, but no one has located him. Wherever he is, he deserves our praise.

Keith (*raises glass*): Here's to Julius Escarriot!
All three raise glasses, drink happily.

Bismark (*checks watch*): Oh, it's time for the news.

All three go quickly to chairs facing TV. Ruth holds up remote control, presses button. Bring lights up on TV side. Each viewer reacts appropriately as TV action unfolds.

Anchor: With us here in the Channel 8 News studio is the winner of the execution lottery, Becky Fordham. (*Turns to* *her*): Congratulations, Becky. That must have been the happiest day in your life!

Becky (*sad look on face*): When I first learned I had won, I *was* very excited. But after the execution, I became deeply sorry that I ever bought a ticket.

Anchor (*surprised*): You're sorry?

Becky: Yes. I attended the execution—a front-row seat was part of my prize. Just before the firing squad began shooting, Jesus prayed for the officers and citizens who were taunting him and for those who were responsible for the execution. He asked God to forgive them—each one of them. I was shocked.

Anchor *puzzled, shakes head.*

Becky: You see, Jesus actually forgave them—he felt no anger, no hatred at all. (*Pauses, speaks slowly.*) He displayed a type of love that I've never even imagined—someone forgiving those who were about to kill him. And one of the other prisoners about to be shot begged Jesus to remember him when he came into his kingdom, and Jesus promised that the other prisoner would be with him in paradise.

Anchor (*snorts*): Paradise, huh? (*Puzzled, uneasy, doesn't know what to do or say*): Well, uh, Ms. Fordham. . . there must be some logical explanation for such odd behavior..

Becky (*rubs eyes*): There is; Jesus is the Son of God, just as he claimed to be. I've never before been so deeply touched by God's love. I dropped to my knees and prayed, and I cried all the way home. The next day, I joined one the worship groups run by his followers.

Anchor (*shakes head*): Well Ms. Fordham, those are your interpretations of events, but let's get back to the facts. After winning the lottery, you immediately left (   ) Square and missed the dance and fireworks?

Becky (*nods*): I went home and prayed all night. The sense of peace that God gave me, and the joy of knowing I had been forgiven, made that night the most restful I have ever had. I discovered that time spent in prayer is far more beneficial than time spent in sleep! (*Smiles, touches her heart with her hand.*) I can still feel the warmth of God's love in the depths of my heart.

Reporter (*very uncomfortable*): Uh, thanks for coming, Ms. Fordham. (*Becky nods, stands, and leaves.*)

Reporter (*shakes head*): You never know what to expect on a live interview! (*Picks up paper, scans briefly.*) We have just received an update on the whereabouts of Julius Escarriot. (*Reads aloud*): "(City) Chief of Police, Larry Benton, today released the report that the body of Julius Escarriot was found hanging from a rope in (   ) Park, three days ago. A note attached to his shirt read, 'I have killed an innocent man—Jesus.' Police suspect foul play and are investigating." (*Puts paper down, continues with news*): Police are also investigating two women who visited the grave of Jesus in (   ) Cemetery this morning and found the grave empty. Extensive investigation reveals that no other persons entered the cemetery following the burial. Chief Benton states that he suspects a hoax—a joke played by some twisted mind. He is also checking out the possibility that somehow one of Jesus' followers removed the body to make it appear that Jesus had come back from the dead as he claimed he would do. (*Picks up a note, reads*): We now take you to Emmaus, where Channel 8 investigative reporter Kevin Richards will interview two local residents.

Recorded voice of Richards: This is Kevin Richards reporting to you from McDougal's Restaurant in Emmaus. Here with me is Paula Jackson, a follower of Jesus. Paula, you call yourself a Chris— how do you pronounce that word?

Recorded voice of Jackson: Christian. It's a new word in our vocabulary. It means a person who believes and obeys Jesus Christ.

Richards: Tell us what happened here in Emmaus.

Jackson (*very excitedly*): My friend Jeff and I were eating here at McDougal's when Jesus came and sat down with us! Jeff is also a Christian, and we were so overwhelmed with grief from the execution of Jesus, that at first, we didn't recognize him. But right there at that table, he broke his sandwich into three pieces, blessed them, and gave each of us a piece! That's when we realized who he was!

Richards (*shocked*): You actually *saw* Jesus and *talked* with him?

Jackson (*nods*): That's right, both Jeff and I saw him. Then he vanished.

Richards: Are you positive the man was Jesus?

Jackson: Absolutely! Jeff and I heard him speak several times! We not only recognized him, we saw a bullet wound in his neck! (*Excitedly*): He is alive! Just like he promised!

Richards: Thank you, Paula. This is Kevin Richards with a Channel 8 live report.

Anchor (*shakes head in disbelief*): I've reported some unusual stories in my day, but this one. . . . (*Puzzled*): Dead, and now alive? (*Pauses, resumes composure*): Stay tuned to Channel 8; as later reports come in, we'll interrupt the regularly-scheduled programs to give you an update on these fast-developing events.

Ruth raises remote control, presses button. Lights go off the TV set and up on the office. The group sits in silence for a few seconds before Bismark speaks.

Bismark (*shakes head*): This is unbelievable!

Ruth (*not too sure of herself*): That was the most preposterous news I've ever heard!

Keith (*hand to forehead, shakes head*): What is making people say these ridiculous things?

Bismark: These claims are not possible—I feel like I'm watching some science fiction show!

Ruth (*shakes head*): I don't know what to think.

Keith: *Could* such a thing actually happen right here in (city)?

Bismark (*angrily*): Don't be ridiculous!

Ruth (*unsure*): Jesus *did* actually predict his death. . . .

Keith (*looks upward, reflecting*): It's all so bizarre. These strange things that are happening make no sense at all.

Bismark: How can a mortal being come back to life after dying?

Ruth (*hesitatingly*): He *did* do some incredible things—I guess you could call them miracles—when he was preaching. It is possible that he really did have power from God? (*Pause, no one answers.*) What other explanation could there be?

Keith (*nods head*): That report you gave about the decline in crime, fewer lawsuits, and healthier people—those things seem to have been the direct result of Jesus' preaching. And I saw him heal Sergeant Dunn's ear after it was cut off. (*Pause.*) It's starting to make sense.

Bismark (*speaks slowly*): He was executed and buried. We know that for sure. Then his grave turns up empty, and now he appears in Emmaus. (*Lowers head.*) Is it possible that these reports were actually true?

Ruth: It's exactly what he predicted—to come back from the grave. We just didn't believe him.

Keith (*nods head*): I should have suspected something when he healed Sergeant. Dunn's ear.

Bismark (*worried*): We may have made a terrible mistake.

The three sit in silence for a moment.

Ruth: We *listened* to what he was saying, but completely failed to hear his message.

Keith: What an awful thing we've done! We've killed an innocent man because he taught love instead of violence.

Bismark (*head in hands*): Love: a power stronger than brute force—what an awesome thing to contemplate! Could it be that this Jesus has power over everything—including death?

Ruth (*choked voice*): We were blinded by our greed, no doubt about it.

Keith (*wipes eyes*): I feel so ashamed.

Bismark: And I'm directly responsible for his death! If only I had believed in him when he was living, it would never have happened. (*Covers face with his hands.*)

Ruth (*voice choked*): There's nothing we can do to correct our terrible error. We had our chance and we blew it. (*Weeps.*)

Keith: And now there's no way we can make it right. Or to be forgiven. (*Looks up for two seconds, then explodes with excitement*): I just remembered something that lottery winner said on TV! (*Bismark and Ruth are stunned by Keith's outburst.*) Just before Jesus died, he asked God to forgive *them*—meaning all those soldiers and people who were taunting him and were about to kill him. That includes us!

Bismark (*excitedly*): That's the only interpretation that makes any sense!
Ruth (*excited*): That's right! He included us as well! We've been forgiven!

Recorded voice from Heaven (*speaks slowly and distinctly*): Each of you is forgiven under God's new covenant of love—the greatest power on earth. All authority in heaven and on earth has been given to me. Therefore go and make disciples of all nations, baptizing them in the name of the Father and of the Son and of the Holy Spirit, and teaching them to obey everything I have commanded you. And surely I will be with you always, to the very end of the age.

All humbly bow their heads.

CURTAIN

A Mother's Love

Characters

Dan Heraldson; pastor, caring and supportive, attired in suit and tie, age 40's
Elinor Howell; caring grandmother, dressed plainly but neatly, age 50-60
Becky Howell; mother, also simply dressed, age 34
Mary Sutton; mother, well-dressed, age 40-50
Theresa Sutton; daughter, average seventeen-year-old, well-dressed
Edward Martin; pastor, kind, well-dressed, age 40-50
Three persons in audience pre-selected to ask questions

Props/Costumes

Seating for five on each side of stage
Bible, magazine, and doll (optional)
Three papers (certificates of recognition)
Clothing fashions to indicate time changes

Scenes

All three scenes take place in the same split-stage setting; the front of a church auditorium, with flashbacks to the living room of the Howell home.

Scene 1: Has a seventeen-year flashback
Scene 2: Has a sixteen-year flashback
Scene 3: Has a four-week flashback

Performance Tips

Split stage. On one side is the front of a church auditorium with five chairs arranged in a slight arc facing the audience. Characters are seated in this order: Becky, Elinor, Dan, Mary, and Theresa. Dan holds a Bible and three certificates. On the other side of the stage is a living room setting, also with seats for five. A doll may be used to play the part of the baby, if you choose to include the baby in scene two.

If special lighting is used, dim and brighten the lights or turn them on and off to signal scene changes.

Scene One: *Lights come up on the church stage as* Dan *stands and approaches the audience.*

Dan: I want to thank all of you for attending our annual Mother's Day Recognition program. This is the 25th year our local churches have sponsored this event, and for the first time, the committee was unable to agree upon one mother who should receive the award. The examples of Christian love expressed by mothers in our community were so numerous that this year, we have selected three mothers for special recognition.

The lives of these three women have become deeply interwoven, and exemplify God's love in action. (*Points to each woman, who nods as her name is called.*) From left to right, we have Becky and Elinor Howell, and Mary and Theresa Sutton. (*Turns back to audience.*) Mother's Day celebrates a very special form and quality of love. (*Holds up a* Bible.) The Bible is our primary source and inspiration for the definition of love. (*Opens* Bible, *reads* 1 *Corinthians* 13: 4-7 *and* 13 *aloud to audience.*)

(*Returns to seat and speaks to* Elinor): Elinor, let's go back to that moment when you first learned about Becky's pregnancy. Would you share with us what happened?

Elinor: Four years after my husband died. Becky, our daughter, was a senior in high school. I worked as a cleaning woman for families here in town. On that small income, I was barely able to keep both of us alive. We have always been poor, but when Ed died, our finances got even worse. We were desperate. (*Glances toward* Becky.) We've often talked about that time.

Becky (*nods*): I'll never forget it as long as I live.

Elinor (*nods*): Nor will we ever forget the day when Becky told me she was pregnant. It was seventeen years ago.

Lights go down or off to indicate a scene change. Becky *leaves the stage, then puts on a sweater or jacket appropriate for a teenager of seventeen years ago.* Elinor *moves to other side of stage, sits down in chair, and begins reading a magazine. Lights come up.* Becky *comes nervously into the room, wringing her hands, and approaches* Elinor.

Elinor (*looks up and becomes concerned at the look on* Becky's *face. Startled, she jumps up*): Becky! What's the matter?

Becky (*begins to weep, is unable to speak.*)

Elinor (*goes to her side, hugs or pats her*): What's wrong?

Becky (*speaks in choked voice*): Mom, I... I've got something to tell you— Oh! I don't know how to say this! (*They sit down next to each other.*)

Elinor: You can tell me anything, Becky. I'll love you no matter what.

Becky (*hesitatingly*): Mom. . . I'm. . . I'm pregnant.

Elinor (*stunned into silence for a moment. Then*): No! Becky! Are you sure?

Becky (*nods*): I'm four months along and the pregnancy is starting to show. I just couldn't tell you before now.

Elinor: How could this have— Who— How could you— Oh! What are we going to do?

Becky (*quickly*): I've decided to have an abortion.

Elinor: Oh, no, Becky. Not an abortion!

Becky: I don't know what else to do. We barely have enough money to stay alive; we can't afford a baby! And I've seen how the kids at school treat the pregnant girls—half of 'em treat them like pieces of dirt and the other half make jokes about having sex! (*Angry and scared*): I just can't take that!

Elinor: Oh, Becky—I'm so sorry. (*Looks up*): Oh, Lord, what can we do? Please help us. (*Bows head, wipes eyes.*) I know we're almost broke, but we'll manage somehow. We must.

Becky (*shakes head*): But Mom, we can't afford to take care of a baby! If I get a job, how will I ever be able to finish school? And what kind of a life can I give to a baby? No one will ever want to marry me!

Elinor: We'll have to face each problem as we come to it, but right now, you're carrying a precious little child who deserves to live. We must do all we can to make that happen—to give it life.

Becky: But how can we, Mom? I want to finish school and get a decent job to help us survive. We don't have either the time or the money for a baby. Don't you see?

Elinor: I assume Eric is the father. He can help support it.

Becky (*shakes head*): I guess you've been too busy to notice that Eric hasn't been around much lately. He says this pregnancy is my problem and refuses to have anything to do with me.

Elinor (*angrily*): But it's *his* problem, too! We can get the court to force him to pay support when he gets a job!

Becky (*tiredly*): I've thought about that. But I hate the thought of having anything more to do with Eric. It would be so much simpler just to have an abortion and get it over with. That way I can finish school and graduate this year. And besides, I hate the thought of all that terrible pain of having a baby.

Elinor (*kindly*): Becky, when did you get to be so selfish? (*Becky look up at her in surprise.*) We're talking about taking the life of a helpless little child. (*Pauses for a moment.*) Some women risk their own lives to give life to a child—just like I did for you.

Becky (*startled*): What are you talking about?

Elinor: I've never told you this before, Becky, because I didn't want you to think you were responsible. But when I was carrying you, I had serious health problems. My doctor gave me a fifty/fifty chance of surviving your birth. He pleaded with me to have an abortion. (*Hand to forehead*): That was the toughest decision I've ever faced. After praying desperately about it, I decided to take the risk of bearing you. God gave me the wonderful opportunity to conceive, and I felt had an obligation to bring you into the world—no matter what happened to me.

Becky (*stunned, shakes head*): You risked your life to give birth to me?

Elinor: Yes, because I felt I had no right to play God. How could I know whose life was more important to Him? As things turned out, God used the experience to teach me a great deal about trusting Him—and your father and I had the great joy of having you and watching you grow. You have always been a very special child because of the circumstances surrounding your birth.

Becky (*in tears, leans over and hugs her*): Oh, Mom! Thanks for giving me life! (*Then looks down, unsure.*) I'd *like* to let this baby live too, but how can I? How can I handle all the pain and humiliation? How would we pay all the medical bills? And how would we be able to take care of the baby after it arrives?

Elinor: We're going to have to put our faith to work, Becky. We'll have to step out and trust the Lord. With His help, we'll find the answers. Somehow, some way, we'll manage.

Becky (*fearfully*): Do you really think we can?

Elinor: I'm certain of it. Why don't we make an appointment to talk this over with our pastor? Maybe he'll have some ideas to help us through. In the meantime, I want you to know that I'm in this all the way—for you and the baby.

Lights off. Becky *removes sweater or jacket, she and* Elinor *move to the other side of stage to original positions.*

END OF SCENE ONE

SCENE TWO: *Lights come up on church setting.*

Dan: Thirty-four years ago, Elinor risked her life to save Becky's. Today (*indicates* Becky), we can see the beautiful result of her life-and-death decision. This is a perfect example of deep, motherly love. (*To* Elinor): For that reason, the committee wishes to honor you on this Mother's Day. (*Hands her a certificate and warmly shakes her hand.*)

Elinor (*nods, smiles*): Thank you for this special honor. God gave me the opportunity to conceive, and I did what I could to give the baby life.

Dan: Even if it meant dying.

Elinor (*nods*): It was not a simple decision, but the experience greatly increased my faith.

Dan (*to* Becky): Tell us about your decision to have the baby.

Becky: At seventeen, all I could think about was graduating and getting a good job. I wasn't ready for the hassle of motherhood—especially without a husband to help me! I was convinced that I wanted an abortion, until Mom told me about risking her life for mine. That touched me deeply. Still, I was really scared. Then we talked to Pastor Dunn. He helped me to see that having an abortion would just increase my guilt—not make my life any easier. He told Mom and me about a local Right-to-Life group that would explain the physical dangers of having an abortion; that really shocked me! We never heard about any of those dangers in school! It made me mad to think about how many of my classmates had had abortions without knowing how dangerous they could be! That's when I finally decided to carry the child to term. Between the Right-to-Life group and the church, I received enough financial help to pay all my medical bills. And my church family was just great! I thought they would turn their backs on me—and, I have to admit that some did. But most were really kind and supportive. Without their prayers and love, I don't know how I would have managed. But, the church really stuck by me and just a few months later, we were blessed with Theresa's birth.

Dan: Tell us what happened after she was born.

Becky (*lowers head, speaks softly*): That following year was the worst I've ever lived. I got a part-time job that paid me just enough to pay a baby-sitter while I was in school. Although Mom did her best to help me, we had one major problem after the other. Money was so tight I had to apply for welfare in order to get formula for Theresa. That hurt. As poor as our family had always been, we never before had to ask for public assistance. And, it seemed to me that Theresa cried all the time. I couldn't get enough sleep to be able to stay awake at school, and I never had time to study. I loved Theresa, but I never had any idea how much work and trouble a baby could be. Dating was out, and to tell you the truth, I was no longer interested in boys. Do you know that Eric never once asked about his baby, and never came to meet her? Even if I'd had the time and the energy to date, I didn't have much interest. (*Pause.*) Before she was born, the counselors in the Right-to-Life center had talked to me about adoption. I rejected the idea because I thought no one could love my baby the way I could—I really believed that! But when Theresa was just about a year old, I went back to the counselors and talked to them again. (*She looks over at her mother.*) Mom didn't know I had done that.

Lights go down or off. Becky puts on her sweater/jacket. She and Elinor go to other side and sit down. If doll is used, Becky may carry it in this scene, occasionally looking into its face, stroking it, etc. Lights come up on the living room/kitchen setting.

Becky (*hand to cheek*): Mom, I've been thinking a lot lately about Theresa's future—and my own.

Elinor: Oh?

Becky: Raising a child is more work that I ever dreamed was possible. (*Elinor smiles and nods.*) I'm too tired to do a good job in school or to be a very good mother. Sometimes I get so angry at that tiny little girl that I'm afraid I'll do something terrible to her!

Elinor: Yes, I know the feeling. But I hope you know you can always come to me when you are feeling like that—no matter what the time of day or night. I' d much rather be called home from work or be awakened in the middle of the night than to have you hurt Theresa.

Becky: Yes, Mom, I know. But you work so hard already that I hate to ask you to do anything more. (*Pause.*) But I've been thinking about more than how tired I am and how hard it is to take care of a baby. (*Pause.*) Theresa will be starting to school in a few years. (*Shakes head.*) I remember how hard it was for me in school because we were poor—I'll never forget the hateful teasing. It seems like someone said something mean everyday: "Why do you wear those ugly clothes?" Or, "I wouldn't be caught dead in those raggedy tennis shoes! (*Drops head.*)

Elinor: I'm sorry you remember those terrible years, Becky. We never had enough money to buy you nice clothes, but I didn't realize the thoughtless comments of your classmates would have such a lasting effect on you.

Becky: Oh Mom, I know you and Dad did your best, but kids can be so mean! I know those things aren't really important, but when you're a kid, it's hard to understand that. Ha! It's hard for me, even now! I see the other girls wearing designer jeans and real jewelry and I get jealous. Then I get mad at Theresa because she's the reason I can't have those things!

Elinor: Are you sorry that you had her?

Becky: No, Mom! Even when I get the angriest with her, I still marvel at what a miracle she is! She's so small and helpless and yet she can be so funny—and so stubborn!

Elinor: Yes, babies are like that! So, exactly what have you been thinking?

Becky: Mom, I went to talk to someone about adoption—do you think that's terrible?

Elinor: Well. . . give me a moment to think; this comes as quite a shock to me.

Becky: Yes, I guess it would. But I've been thinking about it for a long time now. (*Pause.*) Did you know that in the United States there are more than two million infertile couples waiting to adopt a child? And that some of them have been waiting more than ten years?

Elinor: Yes, I've heard those statistics.

Becky: I've been wondering about what kind of a life Theresa might have with me, compared to what she could have with a mom *and* a dad who could give her the things I can't.

Elinor: That's a tough question.

Becky: The part that really bothers me is wondering whether or not someone else could love her as much as I do. But the counselor I talked to showed me some pictures of couples who had adopted babies. Mom, some of those people—men and women—were crying from the happiness of getting a baby! And I saw pictures of the kind of houses they lived in—beautiful houses with cute nurseries and tons of toys. I can't believe people would spend that much money on a child if they didn't really love it a lot!

Elinor: Yes, I'm sure that's true. Couples are carefully screened before they are approved for adoption, and in many cases they are far better prepared and able to provide and care for children than are birth parents.

Becky (*sadly*): Yeah. That's what I found out. (*Pause.*) It's not *just* about money. With adopted parents, Theresa could have a daddy, and maybe brothers and sisters. And she wouldn't grow up with everybody knowing that she's an illegitimate child. And Mom, I even found out that I can ask that she be adopted only by people who are Christians! That way, I'd know that she would be taught about God.

Elinor: It sounds as though you've given this some very careful thought.

Becky (*wipes eyes*): As much as it hurts to even think of giving her up, (*pause*) I just don't see any other way to give her a good life. She *deserves* a better life the she'll *ever* get here with us.

Elinor (*nods, wipes her eyes*): This may be the hardest decision you'll ever have to make, Becky, and I don't want to influence you too much because you'll have to live with your decision for the rest of your life. But it seems to me as if you've weighed your options carefully and that you're coming to a very unselfish decision.

Becky (*hopefully*): Unselfish? Do you really think so? I've been afraid that some of my motives were selfish!

Elinor: In what way?

Becky: I can't see how my own life is going to get any better as long as I have a child to raise. Without your help, I'd have to go on welfare—and I think that's a dead-end street. And how will I ever get the training I need to get a good job? And how will I ever meet a decent man who might want to marry me?

Elinor: Oh honey, it's not selfish to think about your own future—it's wise! You and Eric made a very bad decision when you decided to have sex, and you will live with the consequences of that decision for the rest of your lives. But now you've asked for God's forgiveness and His help; don't you think that He wants you to make something of the rest of your life, and to do the best that you possibly can for Theresa?

Becky (*in tears*): Yes, Mom. And I think that adoption will allow me a second chance of making something of my life, and that it is the very best that I can do for Theresa.

Elinor puts her arms around Becky and they both weep as the lights go down. Becky removes sweater/jacket. Both return origianl positions.

END OF SCENE TWO

SCENE THREE: *Lights come up on the church setting*

Dan (*to audience*): Becky first decided to let her baby live, and later to give her up for adoption. Each of these difficult decisions was made out of love. (*To Becky*): For these reasons, the committee wishes to honor you on this Mother's Day. (*Dan hands her a certificate and warmly shakes her hand.*)

Becky (*with tears in her eyes*): This special honor means a lot to me. Through the years, I've sometimes felt that others thought my decision to place Theresa with an adoptive family meant that I didn't love her, or that I was selfish. Those people don't have any idea how hard the decision was on me—and on Mom. This little certificate says more to me than you'll ever know. Thanks for recognizing that my decision was made out of love for my child, and that although I wasn't able to raise her, I am, and will always be, her mom.

Dan: Thank you, Becky, for helping us to see that there are many ways to love a child. (*Turns to Mary.*) And for our final story today, we will hear from Mary Sutton. (*To Mary*): Would you tell us about the decision you and your husband made many years ago?

Mary: When Tim and I were first married, we decided to wait a few years before we started a family. As it turned out, we learned that we were unable to have any children. After years of medical examinations, treatments, frustration, and dashed hopes, we gave up the idea of having children altogether. However, Pastor Martin urged us to consider adoption. After much soul-searching, we filed our application for adoption with a child placement agency.

Dan: We've heard today that many couples wait for years to receive a child; how long did you and Tim have to wait?

Mary (*smiles*): Seven months. We were extremely blessed to receive a child in that short period of time. Our Theresa came to live with us sixteen years ago; when she was just fourteen months old. (*Excitedly*): It was truly a blessed event in our lives. Many times throughout the years, Tim and I have thanked God for the young woman who decided to bear her child into this world and place her in our home. And, without knowing who that young mother was, we have prayed for her. The child she gave up, (*gestures to Theresa*) this young lady, has brought more love into our lives than we ever thought possible. We've thanked God each and every day for the many blessings we've received.

Dan: Tell us about what happened just three months ago.

Mary: Well, the events that culminated three months ago really began when Theresa was five. Tim and I discussed whether or not to tell her that she was adopted. You see, Tim had also been adopted as an infant. He knew nothing of that until he was fifteen, and a relative accidentally blurted out the news. It came as a terrible shock to him. Because of that experience, he felt that Theresa should be told that she was adopted early in her life. We decided to be right up front about it—out of love for her.

Dan: How did Theresa react to the news?

Mary: When she was too young to understand what the word "adopted" really meant, she understood that it meant she was a very special baby to us, that we waited a long time for her, and felt very happy when we got her. Later, when she was older, she asked about her natural parents. We told her the truth; that we really didn't know anything about them. Then we made a point to shower her with affection. We wanted to make sure she knew she was deeply loved.

Dan: Would you tell us what happened on her sixteenth birthday?

Mary: Somewhere she had read about an adopted child who met his natural parents. On her birthday, she asked if she could also have that opportunity. (*Shakes head*): We had no idea she was interested since she hadn't mentioned being adopted for several years.

Dan: How did you and Tim react to that?

Mary: Well, Tim suggested we look into it. But I was shocked by her request. I wouldn't even consider it.

Dan: Why? What did you think might happen?

Mary: I was afraid that Theresa might love her natural mother more than me. I thought that if I allowed her to meet her birth mother, I might lose my place as her mother altogether. After struggling with those questions for many weeks, we had a long conference with Pastor Martin.

Dan: And what was your final decision?

Mary: I realized that loving Theresa meant thinking of *her* needs—not just my own. I was finally able to step out in faith and trust that God would work things out for the best. I agreed to try to locate her natural parents and Pastor Martin contacted a parent-search group for assistance.

Dan: And what were the results?

Mary: After several months, the researchers were able to determine the names of Theresa's biological parents. Her mother had long ago signed the papers requesting that her name be released if her child ever wanted to make contact. The father had not, and since he had moved from the area ten years ago, they were unable to locate him. However, the mother was still living here in (   ) County. The researchers were very professional about making contact. They made sure that was what Theresa really wanted. They didn't want to force a reunion on her. Pastor Martin acted as a mediator for all of us. He wanted to make sure that Tim and I and Theresa's birth mother felt that meeting was the right thing to do for Theresa's sake.

Dan: What was the conclusion?

Mary: After discussing it separately with each of us—Becky, Theresa, Tim, and I—he was satisfied that each one of us *really* wanted to meet the other. Then he asked us to wait several months more to make sure our individual decisions were firm.

Dan: And finally, you met—a *real* family reunion took place just four weeks ago. Tell us about it.

Mary: As it turned out, Tim was on a business trip so Pastor Martin came with us when Theresa and I went to the Howell residence. Even after all those conferences with Pastor Martin, I was still worried. What if something went wrong?

Dan: How did it go?

Mary (*smiles at* Elinor *and* Becky): I'll never forget that meeting as long as I live. It took place just one month ago.

Lights dim or go off as Elinor, Becky, Mary, *and* Theresa *move to the other side of the stage.* Pastor Martin *enters. All sit down. Lights come up on that side.*

Edward: In my ministry, I've been blessed to witness many acts of Christian love. But this meeting (*smiles*)—maybe I should call it a family reunion—is the most beautiful example of God's love in action that I have ever seen. (*To* Becky): I remember you telling me how grateful you were when you learned that this reunion was to take place.

Becky (*nods, smiles, looks toward* Theresa): Words can't express how excited I was—and am! The opportunity to see Theresa again after all these years seems to me like a miracle. (*To* Theresa): I'm so happy to see you again! It's been sixteen long years. And I want you to know that I prayed for you each and every day—not knowing where you were—and for your new family. It is obvious that my prayers were answered. (*Voice chokes with emotion.*) You're so beautiful, so grown up, such a talented and intelligent young woman.

Theresa (*tearful, looks and smiles at Becky*): I thank God for allowing us to meet! Even though I love Mom (*squeezes Mary's hand*) with all my heart, I've wondered about you ever since I was old enough to understand the word, "adoption." I've been looking forward to this moment for a long time, and yet I was very afraid that you wouldn't want to see me. I didn't want to be disappointed—and I didn't want Mom to be hurt. But now I feel like I have *two* wonderful mothers! (*Stands, runs to Becky who also stands. They kiss and hug.*)

Lights dim or go off. The women return to their original seats in the church setting. Pastor Martin leaves. Lights come up on the church setting.

Dan (*to audience*): And after that first reunion, these two families decided to meet regularly. Mary's act of love means sharing her daughter with another mother—a particularly difficult decision. She was willing to risk losing her daughter to Becky if that's what it took to make Theresa happy. (*Turns to Mary.*) For that decision, the committee wishes to recognize you on this Mother's Day. (*Hands her a certificate and gives her a warm handshake.*)

Mary (*nods, smiles*): I appreciate this very much. (*Pause.*) And I give God the praise. Through His guidance, each of us was able to act in love—for Theresa's sake.

Dan (*to Theresa*): Do you remember when you were first told about your adoption?

Theresa (*nods*): Yes, but I didn't understand what it meant. I'm glad my parents told me when they did however, because I grew up with the knowledge. By the time I understood what "adopted" meant, I was completely confident of their love. It must be very difficult for those kids who grow up thinking they are with their biological parents and all of a sudden find out they aren't.

Dan: And yet, you did wonder about your birth parents?

Theresa: Yes, often. But I think that's pretty natural, don't you? I wondered why they gave me up, or if there was something wrong with me. Whenever those thoughts flashed through my mind, Mom and Dad must have noticed because they would immediately go out of their way to show me just how much they loved me. That was very reassuring.

Dan: Thank you, Theresa. (*To audience*): That concludes our presentation, but our guests have agreed to answer any questions you might have. (*Sees hand raised, points to person.*)

Person #1 (*stands, speaks*): I have a question for Elinor. When you had to decide between having an abortion or the strong probability of dying, didn't you have any fear of dying?

Elinor (*nods head*): At first I did. But after many desperate prayers, I came to believe that the baby must be saved. From that point on, I faced the possibility of death with calmness. After all, death is something that touches each of us at one time or another. And none of us have any guarantee as to how long we are going to live, but as Christians, we do have the promise of an everlasting future. When you consider how fleeting life is in the face of eternity, how much does it really matter when death occurs ?

Person #1 nods and sits down. Dan points to another raised hand.

Person #2 (*stands, speaks*): I'd like to ask Becky a question. After you gave your baby up for adoption, did you have any guilt feelings?

Becky: Guilt? For what reason? My only sin was having sex with Eric, and believe me, I prayed hard to be forgiven for that long before I even told my mother that I was pregnant! After that, thanks to my mother's strong opposition to abortion, I did not commit another sin. The decision to place my daughter in an adoptive home was made to give her a much better life. Although her going left a hole in my heart, I have never regretted the decision. And now, (*gestures toward Theresa*): I'm deeply thankful for the results of that decision—my daughter was raised by a loving Christian family and is a happy, confident young woman.

Person #2: Did you ever wonder about your daughter—where she was, how she was doing?

Becky (*nods, smiles*): Practically every day. Whenever I'd see kids on the school playground, or with their parents at the shopping center, I'd wonder if my little girl was okay. And I would pray for her.

Person #2 sits down. Dan points to another raised hand.

Person #3 (*stands, speaks*): My question is for Mary. Weren't you worried about the possibility of losing your daughter's love to her natural mother?

Mary (*nods*): I think I've already admitted that I was very frightened of that. When I first heard of Theresa's desire to meet her biological mother, my only thoughts were that she must not be satisfied with me and that I would lose her. But Pastor Martin helped me to see that as a very selfish way of thinking. And, he reminded me that love is not a limited entity—we have often heard it said that the more love you give away, the more you have. I had always believed that; now I had an opportunity to put my beliefs into action. Still, I struggled at least three weeks before I could face the idea.

Person #3: Have those worries returned now that you've all met?

Mary: Well. . . not much time has passed since we first met. But I think that I am able to see that there is enough love among us to go around. I see no reason why Theresa and her biological mother cannot be close if they choose to be. Theresa and I are still close. I am still grateful to Becky for making the decision that she did; after all, if she had been more selfish about her unplanned pregnancy, or about losing Theresa's love, I would not have had the sixteen wonderful years with my daughter that I have had! I think that everything has turned out beautifully! (*Gestures toward Theresa, speaks excitedly*): Now Theresa knows that she has two mothers who love her very much. True, we don't know what lies ahead of us, but we have faith that God will help us to handle any problem that may arise. And that's true for everyone—no matter what problems they face.

Person #3 sits down.

Dan (*to audience*): As we learn in 1 Corinthians 13, faith, hope, and love are great gifts indeed. And the greatest of these is love. (*Theresa stands, runs to Mary, hugs her. Then runs to Becky, hugs her. All four stand and walk quickly to front center of stage facing audience with arms around each other.*)

Curtain

Monuments of Success

Characters

Susan Bergman; TV news reporter, confident, age 28-35
TV camera person; voice recorded for playback or performed live offstage
Frederick Metzger; businessman, well dressed, age 50-60
Mary Jones; black, poorly dressed, soft-spoken, age 35-60
Frank Adkins; farmer, poorly dressed, calm, soft-spoken, age 35-60
Pocahontas; Indian, poorly dressed, walks with an obvious limp, age 35-60
Ed Cohen; businessman, well dressed, age 30-60
Elizabeth O'Neil; homemaker, poorly dressed, age 30-60

Props

Six tombstones (wood or poster board) with names and dates of deceased. Each is large enough for character to hide behind until time for his or her lines.

Flowers, flags, other decorations for large stone
Earphone, microphone (or facsimiles)
Cassette with taped voice
Sign: VALLEYVIEW CEMETERY

Scene

Memorial Day in a local cemetery

Performance Tips

Voice that Susan "hears" on her earphones may either be recorded earlier for playback, or performed live offstage (audience also hears it).

Each spirit character hides behind his or her tombstone until time to deliver lines. During the delivery the characters may walk around in front of the stone, sit, or lean on it (if built for such). Following each spirit-person's dialogue, he or she returns to position behind tombstone.

Use lights to signal scene changes.

Scene One: VALLEYVIEW CEMETERY *sign hangs prominantly. As the lights come up Susan is standing at front, center stage, her hand to her ear, listening to a voice on her earphone which the audience also hears.*

Recorded voice: Two minutes to air, Susan. Are you ready?

Susan (*looks toward the rear of the auditorium above the audience*): Would you move the camera back (*motions with her hand*) about ten feet? I want to make sure we get a good shot (*motions behind her*) of the tombstones here in the cemetery.

Recorded voice (*after slight pause*): Okay, we've got 'em now.

Susan: Good. If we open with an overview of the cemetery, the viewers will get the idea.

Recorded voice: Ready to air! Three, two, one-—rolling.

Susan (*drops her hand from her ear*): Good evening. This is Susan Bergman for the XYZ Nightly News, reporting to you live from the Valleyview Cemetery in Metzgerville, (your state). We are here for another segment of our special Memorial Day series on, "Those Who Wrote America's History." As you have probably guessed, we are here to pay tribute to Frederick Metzger, a man whose life has touched thousands of others.

Mr. Metzger (*points to large tombstone*) died April 12, 1896. History books are filled with amazing accounts of his achievements. Born in a log cabin near (local) Creek, he rose above his humble beginnings to set and achieve lofty goals. By the time he was 45, he had been mayor, governor, and a U. S. senator. The impact of his presence upon this community, county and state is clearly evident. His name appears on the local steel mill, a national packing plant, and a railroad line. Both the city and county were named after him, as was the river that crosses the state. As you can see (*gestures hand toward stones*), he has not been forgotten by the local citizens on this Memorial Day.

Fred stands and steps in front of his stone.

This has been Susan Bergman with another episode of— (*sees Fred, screams*) AAAIII! Who . . . who are *you*?

Fred: I'm sorry I scared you. I'm the spirit of Frederick Metzger. I've come from Heaven in answer to your prayer.

Susan (*very sarcastically*): Right! Who are you—*really*? And what—wait a minute—what prayer?

Fred: The one you sent up last night. You see, God allows a few of us senior saints to monitor the prayer channel. And with His approval, we get to answer the prayer requests that we think we can handle.

Susan: What are you getting at?

Fred: Your prayer was most unusual, I must say. You asked God to be with you during this report for some very interesting reasons. You wanted Him to make sure that this special segment got very high ratings because that would mean exposure across the nation—

Susan (*interrupts, very embarrassed*): Uh, that's enough! (*Into microphone*): Uh . . . are we still on the air?

Recorded voice: You bet! Network says this'll knock Cosby clear off the chart!

Susan (*rattled*): Uh . . . right! (*Tries to compose herself.*) Well, viewers, let's see if we can get to the bottom of this interview with . . . (*turns to Fred*): You really must be Jesus.

Fred (*all in a rush*): Oh no, no, no! He won't come down to earth again until later! (*Gestures to other stones*): However, I did bring five other members of the Answered Prayers Department to supply you with several additional facts for your report on my life.

Susan (*puzzled*): What facts did I overlook?

Fred: Back when I accomplished all those things that you mentioned, I thought success meant wealth, prestige, and power. Then, just before I died, I learned a very important lesson; *true* success comes in a different package—wrapped in humility and servanthood and bound together with love.

Susan: I don't understand. Is there a point to all this?

Fred: My point is straight out of Matthew 23, "He who is greatest among you shall be your servant." (*Waves hand around cemetery.*) That means this cemetery is *filled* with successful people. And except for me, not a single one of them was *ever* given any recognition or praise in the media.

Susan (*puzzled*): I don't get it. What do you mean?

Metzger: With me today are five other spirits who will share their life-on-earth stories—each a Christian success story. First, I'd like to introduce Mary Jones who will tell us about her life on earth.

Mary quickly stands and steps in front of her stone.

Mary: Both my parents were born into slavery. After the

emancipation, they were married and moved here to Metzgerville where I was born, At that time, black people were barred from all schools, medical services, public facilities, and all but the most menial jobs.

Susan: How did you manage to stay alive?

Mary: Survival was a day-to-day struggle, particularly since my parents had thirteen children to care for! At the age of fourteen I met Tom and we were married two months later. That made life a little easier on Mom and Dad—one less mouth to feed.

Susan: Was your husband able to find a job?

Mary: He was very fortunate. He got a part-time job at the Metzger Mill sweeping floors. He was the first black to work there; a fact that greatly upset the other workers. But the pay was good—sometimes as much as eight dollars a week.

Susan (*shocked*): How could you live on eight dollars a week?

Mary: We managed a day at a time. After all, eight dollars a week was much better than no income at all. But our happy life together lasted only two years. Then Tom was killed in a furnace explosion—along with eleven other workers.

Susan: How awful! But didn't the company offer to assist in taking care of your family?

Mary (*shakes head*): No, they didn't. I learned that two of the white families asked for help, but were turned down. That's when I knew there was no hope for us.

Susan: Weren't you able to get financial help through the welfare department?

Mary (*shakes head*): Back then, we had no welfare programs or state compensation plans like you have today. And I had no skills, education, and no hope for financial help. We lived by faith from day to day.

Susan (*to Fred*): What's your reaction to that?

Fred (*sadly*): I was completely responsible for the deaths of those men. Earlier that week, I had issued an order for a drastic cut in safety procedures as a way to slash expenses.

Susan: Why were you so eager to increase your profits then that you would endanger your workers?

Fred: That was the year I ran for governor, and campaign costs were sky-high. I was concerned *only* about the bottom line: profit. My life was all *grab* and no *give*.

Susan: Are you suggesting that it's wrong to make a profit?

Fred: No, not at all. The problem is *how* you make that profit, and how you use it. At the time, I was worshiping at the altar of "big bucks." The possibility of deaths as a result of my cost-cutting measures never crossed my mind.

Susan: Did you feel any guilt over those deaths?

Fred: At the time—none at all. Then, in 1895, my doctor told me I had terminal cancer. He gave me less than a year to live. (*Head down.*) That's when I first realized just how far I had strayed from the path on my Christian journey.

Susan: Describe your prior relationship with God.

Fred: Over the years I had faithfully attended church and participated in many of the activities. I even taught a Sunday-school class. But during all that time, I had missed the message completely, and I really had no *relationship* with God. After the doctor's report, I felt the burden of my overwhelming guilt crushing the very breath out of me.

Susan: Did you take any steps to correct what you'd done?

Fred: In desperation, I went to our local pastor and poured out my burden, repenting of my countless sins. He led me back to the Bible and helped me step out in a new direction, in faith.

Susan: Did you notice any changes in your goals and lifestyle after that decision?

Fred: Most certainly. That last year was the most wonderful year of my life, much more meaningful than all the profits, prestige, and power in the world. I spent my last year on earth helping others in every way possible.

Mary: That's when Fred set up a trust fund to construct a private school for blacks and other minorities—all expenses paid. It was the first one established in the country.

Fred: Mary first learned to read and write at the age of twenty-eight. With that education, she became the bookkeeper at the mill.

Susan (*to Mary*): What impact did that have on your life?

Mary: Because of that job, I was able to provide a foster home for several children—and one elderly woman. I introduced each of the children to the Lord and raised them into adulthood.

Fred: Through all those years of persecution, poverty, and hard work, her eternal faith and hope carried her through. (*Very excited*): Now that's *real* success!

Susan: How were you paid for providing those vital services?

Mary (*shakes head*): It didn't cost the children anything, if that's what you mean.

Susan: After all the time and energy you put into their lives, you certainly deserved substantial compensation!

Mary (*shakes head*): It was my way of passing my many blessings on to others in need. (*Hesitates, then*): I was paid in a different form—the deep joy I experienced just watching each child grow into a mature, responsible adult. That was more than adequate compensation!

Susan: Did you hear from any of those children after they left your home?

Mary (*nods, smiles*): Oh, yes—both before and after my death! Since I've been in Heaven, I've heard from many of them over our prayer channel. Just last week, I heard a woman's prayer of deep thanks to the Lord. She was grateful for the fact that her grandmother was able to live with her in my home throughout her teen years.

Susan: Did she explain how having her grandmother there had helped her ?

Mary: Yes. She said that her grandmother's nurturing and examples of faith provided the solid spiritual foundation she needed to step out into the world on her own.

Susan: Do you recall when her grandmother lived with you?

Mary (*nods excitedly*): I certainly do! The child's parents were tortured and murdered by a group of Klansmen—in the presence of the grandmother and the child!

Susan (*shocked*): That's terrible! How old was she at the time?

Mary: She was only twelve. When she and her grandmother came to live with me, she was filled with grief, hopelessness, and raging anger. We surrounded her with warm, Christian love. She was finally able to put that horrible memory behind her, and become a loving Christian woman.

Susan: And it all started when Fred set up that trust fund for a private school for blacks and other minorities?

Mary (*nods*): That's right. When God turned Fred's life around, our community was never the same. The impact of God's love on his heart produced the most amazing results.

Susan: Could you give us any other examples?

Mary: It would take too long to cover them all. I'll just mention one that had an enormous impact on our community. (*Glances toward Fred*): That was the time he violated one of the most rigid, cultural rules in Metzgerville. It occurred right here (*gestures toward headstones*) in Valleyview Cemetery. Ever since the community was first settled, this burial ground was for whites only—no exceptions.

Susan: What did he do to change that?

Mary: Fred's deep Christian convictions compelled him to purchase several burial plots for blacks. That *really* upset the city fathers! There were threats of violence, even rumors that Fred would be killed.

Susan: That's terrible! Were any of those threats and rumors carried out?

Mary (*shakes head*): No, they weren't. Once, several city officials started to dig up a black man's body. But they were stopped before they got very far.

Susan: As you reflect back upon all the pain you suffered, how would you describe it?

Mary (*thoughtfully*): Many verses in the Bible tell us that life on earth is very short, and that since it is, we ought not to be overly concerned with the things of this world. That's very hard to believe until you die and begin to see things from an eternal perspective. I look back on my sufferings as the things that turned me to Jesus, and as the experiences that made me the person I was. I *still* thank the Lord for my countless blessings.

Susan: How can you think of blessings after all you've been through?

Mary: I prefer to focus on the blessings rather than the pain. For example, once I was able to forgive Fred for my husband's death, I experienced a depth of joy and gratitude I'd never known before.

Susan (*puzzled*): You actually forgave him for causing your husband's death?

Mary: As a Christian, I had no choice. The only way we can hope to receive God's forgiveness is to forgive others.

Susan: Thanks, Mary, for sharing your story with us.

As Mary *returns to her original position,* Frank *stands and steps in front of his stone.*

Fred: Now let me introduce Frank Adkins. Frank, Tell us a little about yourself.

Frank: Well, I was born and raised on a tiny farm near the Metzger Mill that my family had owned for many generations. After Betty and I were married, we worked the same farm.

Susan: Was farming your full-time occupation?

Frank (*nods*): Yes, it was. And for most of our marriage, we were barely able to raise enough to feed our family. Then, Fred decided to extend the Metzger railroad through our farm. But we refused to sell.

Susan: What happened?

Frank: He sent several of his thugs out to set fire to our wheat crop. When I ran out to stop them, they beat me with clubs, fracturing my skull, three ribs and shoulder.

Susan: That's terrible! Were they arrested for it?

Frank (*shakes head*): No, they weren't. But I was found guilty on an assault charge and spent three months in jail—just for trying to protect my property and family.

Susan: How can that happen? That's a crime!

Frank: As governor, Fred got whatever he wanted—when he wanted it. He later forced us to sell our farm for less than half the value.

Susan (*to* Fred): What's your response to that!

Fred (*shrugs*): What can I say? At the time, I'd do whatever was required to be "successful."

Susan: Today you could go to prison for such brutality! Did you ever compensate him for those terrible losses?

Fred: Not until five years after it happened, when I finally got my priorities in order. I checked our security department files to be reminded of all the rotten things I'd done over the years. When I came across the record of my employees beating Frank up, I had personnel offer him a blacksmith job. And he accepted.

Frank: I was shocked when I heard about Fred's decision to turn his life around. Betty and I just couldn't believe it. The community was unanimous about his reputation; we considered him a selfish, ruthless, unforgiving tyrant. The job he offered me was the first full-time work I'd had since I lost the farm. I was deeply grateful for that opportunity!

Fred: And Frank's story doesn't stop there. He invited many boys into his home where he taught them the basics of blacksmithing and farming. They learned valuable skills from an expert. Frank also brought them to church.

Susan: Did you ever hear anything about the results of your training program upon their lives?

Frank: Our prayer channel picked up a report this past summer. The prayer was offered at a family reunion and contained a thanksgiving for Don, a family member who had been in our program. Don was praised for his many examples of Christian love that deeply affected the lives of his children.

Susan: Do you recall having him in your program?

Frank (*excitedly*): I sure do! Don was a great kid with a lot of potential. All he needed was a chance. When he got one, he grabbed it and ran with it—became one of the most respected farmers in the area.

Fred: And when you think of the hundreds of other boys who also made a good life for themselves and their families because of Frank's training—you begin to see the *real* success story!

Susan (*to Frank*): You must have made a good living from the profits you made from that training school.

Frank: Profits? No, I didn't charge for my time if that's what you mean. But in a Christian sense, you *could* say it was a profit-maker! Jesus tells us in Luke 6:38 that when we give to others, God will return in equal measure. In my case; I received many times more blessings than I gave.

Susan: Thank you, Frank.

Frank returns to his original position, and Pocahontas stands. She moves in a manner to indicate a crippled leg.

Fred: Now I'd like to introduce you to Pocahontas.

Pocahontas: Because I was an Indian, the white people called me Pocahontas. They didn't know my real name—Red Feathers. I was born in the cave along (   ) River where my parents and six brothers and sisters lived. Then, in 1888 when I was five years old, I left the cave to pick herbs for our family meal. While I was gone, an angry mob of Metzgerville citizens rushed into the cave to kill all of us. When I later returned, I found the dead bodies of my family.

Susan: And you were only five when that happened?

Pocahontas (*nods*): That's right. And I lived in that cave for seven more years.

Susan: Did anybody ever come around your cave again?

Pocahontas: Very few. To them, I was a foreign-speaking witch. (*Chuckles.*) That foreigner tag always made me laugh. My ancestors were here *long* before any of them! Those who did come around called me nasty names like "Crazy Indian." Sometimes they would yell and scream at me. That always scared me. I was afraid they'd come to kill me like they did my family.

Susan: How did you ever manage to exist?

Pocahontas (*shakes head*): Even today when I think back on the horrors of that life, I'm still amazed that I survived. God's hand had to be protecting me.

Susan: Could you give us an example?

Pocahontas: An example of what? The horrors, or how God protected me?

Susan: Either one.

Pocahontas: Well actually, the two usually go hand-in-hand; God works in tragedies, you know. (*Susan nods.*) The best example happened when I was twelve. I was wading in the river trying to catch a fish with my hands when I noticed scum on the water. It came from the Metzger Mill upstream. Suddenly, a fire roared down the surface of the river

Susan: Were you able to get out in time?

Pocahontas (*shakes head*): No, I wasn't. The fire engulfed me, burning my legs terribly. That's how I developed this bad limp. I was lucky I wasn't killed, although the pain was so horrible, I often wished I had died.

Susan: That's terrible! Did anyone come to help you?

Pocahontas: Not for several days. Somehow I managed to crawl to the bank, but that's as far as I got. Pastor Hawkins found me lying on the ground several days later.

Susan: And if he hadn't seen you, you certainly would have died within a few more days.

Pocahontas (*nods*): That's right. I was practically delirious with infection as it was. But after several weeks at the doctor's house, Pastor Hawkins took me home where I was raised as one of his own children. That *had* to be God looking out for me.

Susan: Did you have any problems in the community due your Indian background?

Pocahontas (*nods*): Yes, I did. Several members of Dad's congregation left because he adopted me, but my family stood up for me at all times. I'm deeply grateful for the depth of love I experienced in that home.

Susan: Did the plant officials offer to help in any way?

Pocahontas: Dad pleaded with them to pay my medical bills, but they refused, saying I wasn't their problem.

Susan (*to Metzger*): How could you possibly justify that decision? *Your* company *caused* her disability!!

Fred: At that period of my life, nothing stood in the way of my profits; I was motivated only by greed and selfishness. But, I was reminded of that tragedy several years later as I was checking through our files. That's when I promised God I would do all within my power to help her.

Pocahontas: And that's exactly what he did. He repaid Dad for all my medical costs, and took over the payment of the bills until I was able to walk again, and that included years of therapy. Later I was accepted into his private school.

Susan: Would you tell us how that helped you in life?

Pocahontas: That's where I learned my job skills. Then I was hired for a packing job at the mill.

Fred: I learned that she was the best packer on the line. She performed her duties with total dedication. I later checked the Tithing Department records in Heaven and found that she gave 20 percent of her income to churches and orphanages. That's in addition to donating a large portion of her off-work time to assist immigrants in learning how to read and write.

Pocahontas: Once when I was reading the Bible, I came across Matthew 25:40 where Jesus spoke about helping the "least" of these. Instantly, I recognized my own personal background. I qualified as one of the "least"—at that time, an Indian was considered to be at the very bottom of the social scale.

Susan: That's a beautiful story. Thanks for sharing it with us.

Pocahontas limps behind her stone, and Ed steps in front of his.

Fred: Now let's hear from Ed Cohen. Tell us about your background, Ed.

Ed: I purchased a grocery business in town after Fred had left for the senate. After I arrived, I learned that we were the only Catholics in a very rigid anti-Catholic community. So I kept our religion secret for business reasons.

Susan: Did the townspeople ever learn about your religious connection?

Ed: Not until several years later when I ran for mayor.

Susan: How did they find out about it?

Ed: Unknown to me at the time, the other candidate was one of Fred's closest friends. And Fred was the most powerful politician in this part of the country. His investigators talked with the neighbors in our former community and discovered that we were Catholic.

Susan: What effect did that have on the election?

Ed: Just like in today's scandals, the media impact was unbelievable. The headlines screamed, "DO WE WANT A CATHOLIC MAYOR?" I was defeated by a landslide.

Susan: Did the news also effect your business?

Ed: It devastated me. The day that headline appeared, the citizens boycotted the store. I was finally forced into bankruptcy and left Metzgerville forever.

Susan (*to Fred, angrily*): What's your response to that?

Fred (*lowers head*): Guilty. People with political power are particularly susceptible to using it ruthlessly. The temptation to control the lives of others is one of the most devious spinoffs of success; you don't even realize it's happening.

Ed: Then, after Fred's decision to follow Christ, he bought me a store in a nearby community. He even loaned me enough money to stock it—interest free. I can't find the words to properly express my gratitude for the impact of that spiritual change in Fred's life. Because of the new direction in his life, my family and I were able to start over.

Fred: As a direct result of Ed's experience of living in poverty, he arranged for a special account with a clothing store owner. He funded an anonymous charge account for families living in poverty. Both teachers and pastors referred people to that store for whatever they needed. Ed received a bill each month which he promptly paid. And before Ed's death, he set up a trust account to continue paying those bills for another thirty years.

Susan (*incredulous*):He provided all that money for total strangers without expecting any repayment?

Fred (*nods*): That's right. Those families never knew where that money came from.

Susan (*to Ed*): Didn't you at least get some newspaper credits to boost your business sales?

Ed (*shakes head*): No, I didn't. Jesus told us in the Sermon on the Mount to give anonymously.

Susan: Thanks, Ed, for sharing with us.

Ed returns to his original position, while Elizabeth steps in front of her stone.

Fred: Now I'd like to introduce you to Elizabeth O'Neil. Tell us something about your background, Elizabeth.

Elizabeth: My story starts in 1891. My husband Art was working at the mill when the American Federation of Labor tried to organize the plant. Art and a large group of coworkers picketed at the gate. It was a peaceful demonstration; they simply carried signs. However, without any warning whatsoever, the mill guards swarmed out of the building and fired at them from a distance of twenty feet.

Susan (*stunned*): That's terrible! Was your husband injured?

Elizabeth: He was killed, along with twelve others. It's still known today as the "Metzgerville Massacre." Thirteen widows were left penniless, and without job skills.

Susan: Thirteen defenseless people—murdered! (*To Fred*): How do you explain that?

Fred: Again, I was personally responsible for those deaths. At the time, I interpreted that union challenge as an attempted takeover of my business. Today, those shootings would qualify me for the death penalty.

Susan: Did you feel any remorse over what you'd done?

Fred: I'm sorry to say I had none. At the time, I felt it was completely justified. After I turned my life over to the Lord, and found that tragic report in the company's records, I recalled the Bible story about King David who planned the death of Bathsheba's husband. Suddenly, the truth hit me. I had caused the death of thirteen innocent workers. My crime was even worse than King David's.

Susan: And what did you do about it?

Fred: I fell to my knees, tears streaking my face. The weight of that terrible guilt was overpowering. I asked God to please forgive me, to take away that enormous burden. As I prayed for help, I felt that weight slowly lift and I knew exactly what I had to do. I went immediately to the homes of the widowed women and apologized for the worst sin I'd ever committed. I begged for their forgiveness. I told them I knew there was no way to bring their husbands back, but I promised to spend the rest of my life helping them in every possible way I could.

Elizabeth: And he did exactly that. He set up a trust fund for those left without wage earners. My children and I received living expenses as well as free job-training.

Fred: And after Elizabeth's death, her granddaughter was so deeply touched by her story, she volunteered to assist women who had been widowed, divorced, or battered. Just like the Bible promises us, God's love goes on and on.

Elizabeth (*nods*): That's right. It multiplies when it is shared with others. But love simply can't survive if kept to oneself.

Fred: And there we have the success story of another Christian.

Susan: I think I'm finally getting your point. Until now, this particular definition of success never occurred to me.

Fred: I'd much rather be remembered for what happened after God touched my heart, than—

Susan (*happily interrupting*): With our national TV coverage, I can almost *guarantee* that you will be remembered in a different way! We may also have to re-write our history books. I've been deeply touched. You've certainly given me an education today!

Fred (*gestures to cemetery, speaks to audience*): These tombstones represent monuments to *real* success—the kind not measured in wealth, prestige, or power. What these people needed to achieve that kind of success was *spiritual* help. During our lives, any of us can tap into the same source of support and assistance that they did, so that we may also become an example—a monument, if you will, for others to respect and emulate. (*Pauses, reflecting, then gestures toward audience*): The Lord offers us more than salvation. When we accept Him into our hearts, He promises to help us. Simply by accepting that help, and by striving to be obedient to Him, we can each leave behind "A monument to success."

Susan This is Susan Bergman reporting from Valleyview Cemetery in (city, state) for XYZ Nightly News.

CURTAIN

Remembering Father

CHARACTERS
Lori Harden; daughter, loving, sensitive, age 20-25
Rick Harden; slightly older brother, understanding, kind
Phyllis Harden; mother, sensitive, caring, age 40-60
Jack Harden; father, businessman, aggressive, overpowering
Jack's Conscience; May be played by another person live on or offstage, or may be Jack's or another person's voice prerecorded for playback.

SCENES
Scene 1: Table in restaurant
Scene 2: Eight-year flashback to kitchen of wealthy family
Scene 3: Same table in restaurant

PERFORMANCE TIPS

The play will be performed on a stage split between two scenes: a restaurant, and a family kitchen.

For scene two, Lori and Rick put on "younger" clothing (a jacket or sweater) to indicate a passage to an earlier time. Also, Lori adds a cast to one leg and uses crutches. Lori and Rick return to their original outfits for scene three. Each of the characters carries a handkerchief for use when needed.

Use lights to signal scene changes.

PROPS

Beside whatever kitchen and restaurant props you choose to have, you will need:

A table and chairs for two on each side of stage
Coffee cups or drinking glasses, and a photo album
Three handkerchiefs
A cast for Lori's leg, and crutches
Sign: QUINN'S RESTAURANT
Prerecorded voice (unless Conscience is played live)

SCENE ONE: *Lori is seated in the restaurant, sipping her drink. There is a beverage at the empty chair, and a photo album on the table. After a moment, Rick enters and walks to her table.*

Rick (*excited, grinning*): Hi, little sister!

Lori (*excited, stands, arms outstretched*): Hi, Rick! (*They embrace, then take seats.*)

Rick: It's been a long time—too long.

Lori (*nods*): That's for sure. We're just too far apart to visit very often. (*Points to beverage*): I went ahead and ordered (   ) for you.

Rick: Thanks, Lori. (*Takes a sip.*) I'm certainly glad I caught you at home when I called this morning. I decided to take the day off work to visit you and Mom.

Lori: Your timing was perfect. I always take a break around ten o'clock, so meeting you here works out perfectly. Will you be able to spend any time with Mom?

Rick (*nods*): I called her before I left. She's at a church meeting until noon or so. Since it's Father's Day weekend, I thought we could pick up Mom, have lunch, and then visit Dad's grave for a few minutes.

Lori: Good idea. I'll meet you in front of my building at noon.

Rick (*points to album*): What's that?

Lori: It's our family photo album. I borrowed it from Mom last week, and then after you called, I thought I'd bring it along so we could look through it. It should bring back some memories of the years past, and be a chance to remember Dad—just in time for Father's Day.

Rick: Great! A perfect opportunity! (*Looks toward the album.*) I haven't looked at that for several years.

Lori opens album.

Rick: Look! My sixth birthday party. That was *the* big one—just before I started first grade. (*Pokes her with his elbow*): And there *you* are blowing out *my* candles before I had a chance to! (*They laugh.*)

Lori (*points*): Here's my Sunday-school class picnic—and me with a mouth full of food! Mom was always taking my picture at the wrong time. (*Both laugh.*)

Rick (*points*): I had forgotten about parents' day at the scout camp. (*Chuckles.*) Mom always made sure my life jacket was properly fastened before our canoe ride. (*Points*): Look!

There you are at your Girl Scout party!

Lori (*smiles ruefully*): That was the time we had to introduce our parents to the others. I was *so* embarrassed, since only Mom was there. Dad was on a sales trip.

Rick (*points*): Oh! Remember that time we rode the Crazy Demon ride at the state fair? (*Excited*): *Look* at you! You're hanging onto me like you were scared to death!

Lori: I *was* scared to death! Anyway, that's what big brothers are for—to protect little sisters! (*Nudges him with her arm.*)

Rick (*grins*): At the time, I was sure you were going to cause us both to fall off the ride! (*Both explode with laughter.*)

Lori: Look, there you and Mom are, playing catch out back.

Rick (*studies it closely.*) Mom really gave her all for us, didn't she? Even playing ball with me.

Lori (*puzzled*): When I thought about celebrating Father's Day by looking through these photos, I'd forgotten Dad was never around. He was always out of town.

Rick: Or had to work. But Mom filled in for him every time.

Lori (*points*): There's another one—my YMCA swim contest.

Rick: Mom and I were so proud of you—first place winner. (*Pats her on back.*) And Dad couldn't make it. He had a meeting somewhere.

Lori (*turns page, gets suddenly serious*): Oh! I'll never forget all the time I spent in the hospital after my car accident!

Rick (*shakes head*): The doctor told us there was little hope of saving your leg. That was really hard to take. (*Examines photo closely.*) But Mom stayed with you at the hospital for three weeks—praying constantly. She slept right there in the chair. (*Hesitates.*) Did Dad ever get around to visiting you there?

Lori: Just once. He was somewhere out of town opening a new plant for the company. (*Sees another photo*): That's the day I came home from the hospital! Mom's pushing me down the hospital ramp. (*Looks up*): For the next four months, she pushed me everywhere.

Rick: Yep, she was always there when we needed her. (*Turns page of album, points*): Even for my football games. At the time, I was jealous of my friends. Both of their parents attended all their activities. For us, it was only Mom.

Lori: Except that one afternoon when Dad took us to (nearby amusement park). But even then he spent nearly two hours on the phone talking to the people at the office. (*Sighs.*)

Rick: At that time, his only goal in life was to be CEO of his company—he would do whatever that required.

Lori (*sadly*): And he made it; the position was finally offered to him just eight years ago. I'll never forget the exact moment he told us about the company's decision!

Rick (*nods*): I can still see the excited look on his face as if it were yesterday. (*Looks upward.*)

END OF SCENE ONE

SCENE TWO: *Lori and Rick change into clothes that indicate they are still in high school and Lori gets a cast on her leg. Lights come up on kitchen scene. Phyllis is alone at the table holding a glass or cup and staring straight ahead as if in a daze. After a moment, Rick enters.*

Rick (*goes to table, sits down*): I thought I'd check on Lori to make sure she's okay.

Phyllis (*looks at Rick*): Is she sleeping comfortably?

Rick (*nods*): Yes, she is. That pain medication must be working.

Phyllis: I just heard from her doctor. He's scheduled her third surgery for Friday morning. (*Sighs, wipes eyes with handkerchief.*) He says there is still a strong possibility she'll lose her leg.

Rick That's hard to believe, after all this time.

Phyllis: She needs our prayers badly. And Dad, too.

Rick (*puzzled*): Pray for Dad? Why?

Phyllis: Do you remember him talking about the possibility of being promoted to chief executive officer?

Rick (*nods*): Yes, I remember.

Phyllis: Well, the board was to meet today to select a new CEO. (*Checks watch*): They should have decided by now. If they choose your father, we'll have to move to (city 1000 miles away) within a few weeks. (*Continues dabbing at tears.*)

Rick: I just can't believe Dad would do that to us! It's the worst possible time for Lori, and I'm not too crazy about the idea myself!

Phyllis: I know. We'll just have to pray he doesn't get the promotion.

Rick (*sighs heavily, stands to leave*): We just *can't* leave now! I can't handle it! (*Walks from the room.*)

Phyllis (*head bowed*): Oh, Lord, I desperately need Your help to get through the next few hours. Please help Jack realize what a terrible impact moving would have on the kids. (*Looks up, wipes eyes, stares blankly. Continues staring as Jack enters.*)

Jack: I got it! (*Kisses her lightly on the cheek, begins to baost.*) I'm the new CEO! (*Hesitates, touches her shoulder.*) Hey! Did you hear what I said? I got the promotion! (*Fails to notice her lack of response, parades around with appropriate gestures.*) I'm the boss over 850 employees! Now I'll start getting the respect I deserved all along! (*Slaps hands together*): Ninety grand a year! Unlimited expense account! A company car! (*Sits down.*) I start to work in (same city as before) on the (date). Let's see, that gives us two weeks to pack up and take off! I can't wait! (*Grins, slams fist to table.*)

Phyllis drops her head onto her arms on the table and weeps.

Jack (*fails to notice her*): I called our Realtor as soon as I heard the board's decision. He'll get the house on the market tomorrow. Then I'll fly out to (city) and line up a house to buy. With all that money, we can—(*Finally notices her*): Phyllis! What's wrong? Are you ill?

Phyllis (*slowly raises her head*): I can't believe it.

Jack (*puzzled*): You can't believe what?

Phyllis: That you'd do this to Lori and Rick.

Jack (*upset*): What are you talking about?

Phyllis: You have no idea what this move will do to them!

Jack (*offhandedly*): Oh, don't worry about them; they're tough. They'll be able to handle it. Changing schools is no big deal. And besides—

Phyllis (*interrupting*): You haven't the slightest idea what they're going through right now! Or the impact that moving would have on their lives!

Jack: Your trouble is you worry too much. Look, school is about out now anyway, so—no problem. Like I said, they're tough kids. Don't you see? They can handle it.

Phyllis: Have you forgotten about Lori's leg?

Jack (*puzzled, shakes head*): Of course not! But what's that got to do with my promotion?

Phyllis: She's still on crutches. Just like she was the last time you were home—two weeks ago!

Jack: I'm aware of that. So?

Phyllis: She's in so much pain now, she spends most of her time in bed. And she's scheduled for surgery again on Friday! For the third time!

Jack (*waves his hand*): That's no problem. She'll be walking by moving day.

Phyllis: Jack! She's in danger of losing her leg! Doesn't that concern you at all?

Jack (*shakes his head*): She'll make it, she's tough. (*Looks up, reflecting*): I think I'll call the moving company.

Phyllis (*bows head, sniffles as she talks*): How can you be so selfish? (*Head still down, sniffles as Jack talks to himself.*)

Jack (*fails to hear her, walks around room as he talks*): I'll line the movers up for the (   )th. That way we can pull out of here in time to arrive there before the (   )th.

Phyllis (*angrily*): You haven't heard a thing I've said!

Jack (*looks at her, surprised*): About what?

Phyllis: You're impossible! I've been talking about Lori now for the last ten minutes.

Jack: Well, what about her?

Phyllis: It's critically important that she stay with the same doctor until she recuperates! And her psychological well-being is just as important to her recovery as physical care.

Jack: Well, there's *no* way we can stay here after the (   )th!

Phyllis: Doesn't she mean anything to you at all?

Jack: Of course she does!

Phyllis: What about Rick? Aren't you concerned about him?

Jack: Not at all. He's strong enough to handle a move.

Phyllis: Don't you remember that he was picked to be captain of the football team next year? And that he has a good chance of being selected for the all-conference team?

Jack (*first perplexed, then happy*): Ah . . . yeah, that's right.

Phyllis: Well, if we move, he'll miss out on both of those opportunities!

Jack: Oh, well . . . don't worry about Rick. He'll make the team at his new school.

Rick and Lori enter, Lori on crutches with leg in a cast.

Rick and Lori: Hi, Dad.

Jack (*excited*): Hi, kids! You know that promotion I've been aiming for? (*Presses thumb to chest*): I got it! You're looking at the new CEO!

Lori and Rick are stunned, stare at Jack, speechless.

Jack: Well, come on, say something! This is the moment I've been waiting for! This represents years of hard work!

Rick (*speaks flatly without emotion*): Congratulations, Dad. I know that job means a lot to you.

Jack: It also means we've hit easy street! We're gonna be somebody in (new city). We'll have prestige and power, and more money than we'll have time to spend! We're moving in two weeks! (*Claps hands*): Isn't that great?

Lori and Rick (*upset, in unison*): No! (*Lori begins to cry.*)

Rick: Can't we at least wait until Lori's gotten over her surgery? Or until football season is over?

Jack (*shakes head*): Not to worry! You'll be at your new school in time to practice with the team there.

Rick (*angrily*): But what about Lori's surgery?

Jack: No problem. She'll be up and around by moving day.

Rick (*shakes head*): You just don't get it, do you, Dad?

Lori and Rick wipe their eyes as they angrily leave the room.

Jack (*puzzled*): What's wrong with them?

Phyllis (*very angry*): You've just ruined their lives, Jack! They're shattered! And you don't even care!

Jack (*angrily*): I've worked myself to death for you (*jabs finger toward door*) and those kids! Nobody appreciates my sacrifice! I expected a celebration! But all I get is a funeral!

Phyllis rises quickly, starts toward exit.

Jack (*grabs her arm, holds her back as he shouts*): Everything you've ever gotten came from me! And don't you forget it!

Phyllis (*very angry*): Sure! You've bought me plenty of *stuff*! But what I really want from you can't be bought! What about your time and attention? What about your love? All you ever think about—all you ever *care* about is your precious job!

Jack: What do you want from me?

Phyllis: Just a tiny part of your day would be a good start! We've *never* gotten your full attention! Or your love! (*Turns head away from Jack.*)

Jack stands silent, perplexed. Phyllis is also silent until she turns back to Jack.

Phyllis (*speaks with a new strength in her voice*): I'm staying here until Lori has fully recovered! And until Rick has graduated. (*Jerks loose.*)

Jack (*raging anger*): But you can't do that! Think of my company image!

Phyllis: All I've ever heard from you is your company image! What about a loving image to your family for a change? (*Short pause.*) Look, it's not too late. Turn down that offer and keep your present job!

Jack (*shakes head*): No way! And besides, they've already hired my replacement.

Phyllis: Fine! But I'm staying here until Lori's condition stabilizes and Rick graduates. Maybe you'll find time in your *busy* schedule to attend *that* event! (*Stalks from the room.*)

Jack (*gestures angrily, paces floor while speaking*): I can't believe this! Why is she doing this to me? After all I've done for her! (*Gestures upward with hands*): I bought her this mansion! A new car every three years! Diamonds! Furs! (*Frantic rage on face as he marches round the room.*) After fourteen years of climbing the corporate ladder—this is what I get! (*Sits down, head in hands.*) What have I done to deserve this?

Jack's Conscience: Do you really want to know?

Jack (*stunned upon hearing voice, or seeing person*): What— what— who said that?

Conscience: Don't be alarmed.

Jack: Who are you?

Conscience: I'm your Christian conscience.

Jack (*grimace on face, stares toward audience*): This is weird.

Conscience: You've ignored me for most of your adult life, to the point that I almost gave up. But occasionally, your early church training shines through.

Jack: I don't understand. What do you want?

Conscience: To try to answer your question.

Jack (*puzzled*): What question?

Conscience: The question you asked a few minutes ago. You said, "What have I done to deserve this?" So if you're ready and willing, I'll try to answer.

Jack: The last thing I want is a needling conscience.

Conscience: Hey! You asked what you'd done to deserve this. A full explanation would take at least a week, but I'll make it easy on you—I'll just cover a few of the highlights. Then you can decide if you need some assistance.

Jack (*looks away, aggravated*): Okay, fire away!

Conscience: Phyllis mentioned the family's need for love.

Jack: But I gave them all the luxuries of life! What more do they want?

Conscience: *Real* love, Jack! Your time, a listening ear and a deep concern for everything that happens to them. That's what love is all about.

Jack: Look, I gave them all the time I could spare! We have only twenty-four hours a day, you know!

Conscience: We're talking about a very small percentage of your total time. This past year, except for sleep time, getting ready for bed and work, and breakfasts, you averaged twelve hours a month at home. That calculates out to twenty-four minutes per day—and most of *that* time was spent in front of the TV, or on the phone. And you attended church only two times all year: Easter and Christmas.

Jack: But what about the money I gave to the church—and spent on my family! Doesn't that count for anything?

Conscience: Certainly. Sharing your income with others is very important. But the Scriptures tell us that the love of money is the root of all evil. Worshiping money leads to ruined lives. By contrast, the Bible is filled with examples of the right kind of love. In 1 Corinthians 13, Paul speaks of love as being patient, kind, and forgiving. That requires a listening ear, an attentive mind, and a caring heart.

Jack: But I did listen to her—just a few minutes ago.

Conscience: You may have listened, but you didn't *really* hear. You completely missed Lori's and Rick's anguish. When they left heartbroken, you asked Phyllis, "What's wrong with them?" You were boastful, arrogant, rude, and insisted upon your own way. Paul clearly states that those attitudes are directly opposed to love.

Jack: Are you suggesting I don't love my family?

Conscience: I'm talking about showing how much you love them. In addition to listening and hearing them, try laughing and crying with them. Or hugging them, or just patting them on the back. Those are simple actions that express love.

Jack: When I first arrived home today, I kissed Phyllis. Then I touched her shoulder. Don't those count?

Conscience: Certainly, but those touches would have had a real impact on Phyllis if you had meant them. You weren't showing love for her, you were simply re-directing her attention to you and your achievements. All you talked about was your newly-won power, prestige, and money.

Jack (*looks toward audience, sullen*): And what's wrong with making money? My family has to eat, you know!

Conscience: I'm talking about your motive. Do you recall the parable of the rich young man in the Bible?

Jack (*nods*): Yes, I recall it.

Conscience: That man worshiped money—it was his god. And because of that, he chose to lose his salvation. Jesus calls us toward a higher standard of living; to let all of our actions be centered in love. He set the perfect example with his concern for all kinds of people: the crippled, blind and deaf, even the untouchables—the lepers.

Jack (*hesitates, then*): That's right, He did.

Conscience: And the people that Jesus helped weren't even family, or close friends. Jesus showed His love for everybody.

Jack (*hesitates, reflecting*): It's been so long since I've been in church, I had forgotten that fact. They *were* total strangers to Jesus. (*Pauses.*) And none of them was rich or powerful.

Conscience: That's right, just everyday people. If Jesus showed such deep love for strangers, shouldn't we at least do the same for our immediate families?

Jack (*pauses*): Well . . . I guess you're right. But after seeing the hateful way Phyllis treated me and the kid's reactions to my promotion, (*throws up hands in despair*) it's probably too late.

Conscience: Jack, it's never too late. You haven't lost them yet, only driven them further from you. They've forgiven you countless times over the years.

Jack (*surprised*): Forgiven me? For what?

Conscience: It would take several days to name all the times you've disappointed and hurt them. I'll give you only a few examples. You failed to attend *any* of your children's school functions, scouting events, church programs, YMCA activities, or birthday parties.

Jack puts hand to forehead, bows head slightly.

Conscience: And you were always "too busy" to take them sledding, or swimming, or anywhere. Whenever they asked you to take them someplace, you refused—and their spirits were usually crushed.

Jack drops head into both hands.

Conscience: You need to be forgiven for failing to notice and appreciate your wife's special homemaking and child-rearing abilities. She's one the most loving wives in the world—a blessing you don't deserve. And you've been completely unaware of that for over nineteen years now.

Jack (*sighs deeply into hands, looks up, pleading*): But what can I do about that now? (*Listens intently throughout the following, nods where appropriate.*)

Conscience: First, you must admit your wrongdoings. Then pray for the courage to apologize to your family and ask their forgiveness. Then you've got to reorganize your priorities. How much of your life are you going to give to God? Do you love your wife and children? If so, how are you going to show them? Ask yourself, "What will I have if I gain the whole world and lose my soul?"

Jack (*shakes head, speaks slowly and softly*): Absolutely nothing.

Conscience: Jack, if you decide to put your family first, that decision will mean a totally new direction in your life. I know you can do it. (*Pause.*) I'll be quiet now, but I want you to know I'm on call—anytime you need my help.

Jack (*elbows on table, bows head, hands on forehead*): Oh, Lord, help me. Please help me. I've been avoiding You for many years now, living in total darkness. I've been worshiping money. And power. And I didn't even realize it. I always thought that fathers showed love for their families by buying them fancy gifts—the more expensive, the greater their love. (*Hesitates.*) But I was dead wrong. (*Shakes head.*) I've hurt Rick and Lori deeply. (*Sighs*): Through the most important years of their lives, I was just too busy to care, to give them even a few minutes of my time. (*Sighs, wipes eyes.*) What a terrible thing to do. And no way to change those events, or make up for all those lost years. (*Three seconds of silence. Then, surprise in voice*): And yet, Phyllis and the kids hung right in there! They *showed* how much they cared for me by their patience and forgiveness! Even though I didn't deserve it. (*Sighs.*) Lord, please give me the courage to apologize to each of them, and to ask their forgiveness. Help me find the proper words to express my love for them. Lord, I'm going to step out in faith, trusting You to help me straighten out my priorities from now on.

END OF SCENE TWO

SCENE THREE: *Rick and Lori return to their original clothing, Lori removes the cast. Lights come up on the restaurant set. Throughout their dialogue, Rick and Lori look at the album and occasionally sip from their glasses.*

Rick (*happy, excited*): Did Mom ever tell you what happened after we left the kitchen that day?

Lori (*shaked head*): I don't think she knows! We heard them yelling at each other, but they had done that before. . . and Mom's yelling certainly never had such an impact on Dad before. . . he was like a different man that evening!

Rick: That's a good description. From that day on, we had a new father!

Lori: I'll never forget what happened when he came back into the kitchen. The three of us were sitting there, overwhelmed with grief from his decision to move away—

Rick (*interrupts*): And he came in and actually hugged each one of us! Something he'd never done before!

Lori: And then he *apologized* for his selfishness and asked for our forgiveness!

Rick: I was so stunned, I couldn't speak!

Lori: Rick, that was the most beautiful moment I've experienced in my entire life.

Rick: Yeah. (*Sighs.*) Things sure changed after that.

Lori (*turns a few pages of the album, stops*): Here we are at the church family potluck, just a few weeks later. (*Points.*)

Rick: (*grins.*) Look at that smile on his face!

Lori (*laughs*): He was the center of attention—everyone wanted to welcome him back to church!

Rick: He said he felt like the prodigal son in the Bible! And he was a faithful member from that day on. (*Points to other photo*): There he is on our weekend camp-out at (   ) Park. Look at him laughing; he thoroughly enjoyed that weekend.

Lori (*looks at Rick, smiles*): Remember when we heard him tell Mom how much he appreciated her homemaking and child-rearing skills over the years? Then he hugged and kissed her and told her how God had blessed his life.

Rick: He even cooked our meals—every one of them. He said he was doing it to give Mom a much-needed rest from all her homemaking duties.

Lori (*points to photo*): There's Dad walking me as part of my physical therapy. During my recovery, he insisted that I walk around the block with him several times each day. For me, it was too much hassle trying to walk on those crutches. I just wanted to stay home and watch VCR tapes.

Rick: But he kept after you—day after day. I felt so sorry for you during those months. It didn't seem fair to me.

Lori: But he was right! Because of him, I was able to walk without those crutches within eight months. And that summer, I started swimming at the pool. Without Dad's insistence, I might still be on crutches!

Rick (*points to photo*): There he is again at my last football game. He never missed a single one during my senior year! I can't describe how good it felt to know Dad was out there in the crowd—I think I played better than I ever had before!

Lori (*shakes her head*): I'm still amazed when I think of the incredible faith and courage it took for him to resign his position as CEO and take that job with the city.

Rick (*nods*): He took a huge cut in pay and prestige.

Lori: But because he had fewer responsibilities, he had time to become active in the church.

Rick: And with us. For the first time in our lives, he was willing to do things with us.

Lori (*nods*): The change in him was truly amazing, Rick, but the part that impressed me the most was Dad's new attitude toward money! He insisted on tithing—even though we were already living on less than we ever had. He said sharing his material blessings with others was the least he could do to show his gratitude to God. (*Shakes her head.*) And he never quit! I've followed his example ever since.

Rick: I had never heard about tithing time and skills until Dad started doing it. With his many years of business experience, he started the "Feed My Sheep" program at church.

Lori: Remember all the time he spent teaching you how to run the program? He was so patient, and so encouraging!

Rick (*nods*): How could I ever forget? Without his help, I wouldn't have had the confidence—or the faith—to even get involved.

Lori: And the program wouldn't have had you as a leader

after Dad died.

Rick (*nods*): That's exactly right.

Lori: And just think of the thousands of people whose lives have been directly affected by that program.

Rick (*nods*): Dad liked to call the program, "Christian love in action." I guess that's what we saw in him throughout those last years. (*Pause.*) I'm so grateful for the time we had together.

Lori: Every hour he spent with us, every time he hugged me, I felt years of frustration and loneliness slip away. (*Glances at photo album, points*): There's the camper Dad rented for our trip to the ocean.

Lori and Rick sit in silence for several seconds, shaking their heads.

Rick: It's hard to even think about that camper. (*Wipes eyes.*)

Lori (*Wipes eyes*): Dad had gone to pick up some milk for lunch. Mom, and you and I were caught inside when the gas stove exploded, and we were pinned beneath the table. That's when I passed out.

Rick: The next thing I knew, Dad was there pulling each of us out from under the table, and pushing us outside. The explosion of the propane tank trapped him inside. (*Choked voice.*) He never made it back out.

Lori: Before the change in Dad, do you think he would have risked his life to save ours?

Rick (*shrugs*): I don't know. I was never sure that his love for us was very deep. But, before the change, we would never even have been on that trip—maybe Dad would still be alive.

Lori (*closes album, looks up*): The way he was? I'm not sure I'd call that living. I'm just grateful that Dad found his life before he lost it.

Rick (*hesitates, reflecting, then*): Yes, our memories of those few good years together will stay with us forever—particularly as we celebrate Father's Days.

Rick and Lori smile and nod as the lights go down.

CURTAIN

In a Foreign Land

CHARACTERS

Sue; wife, sensitive, casual attire, age: 25-40
Gary; husband, grumpy, casual attire, age: 25-40
Alan Griffin; TV reporter, age: 25-40
George Washington, John Quincy Adams, Thomas Paine; businessmen of the 1700's, attired in period costume, ages 50-65
General; stern, in Army uniform, age 30-40
Frederick the Perfect; dictator, pompous, wears a crown and flowing robe, age 45-60
Servant; formal attire, humble, age 20-30
Three men and three women who ask questions. These actors/actresses will be sitting out in the audience.

SCENES

Scene 1: Living room in home
Scene 2: TV set/studio
Scene 3: Later, in the same living room

PROPS/SETTINGS

Split stage. Living room setting on one side, and a TV set/studio on the other. Living room contains two chairs or a sofa angled toward the TV set/studio and the audience. A coffee table or end table contains a remote control, a newspaper, and a TV *Guide*. The TV set/studio contains a place to display a map in the rear, four chairs in front of that angle toward the living room set and the audience, a table in front of the chairs containing another remote control, notebooks, a coffee pot, cups and napkins, and a cassette player. A sign on the wall proclaims, "XYZ NETWORK."

Necklace with large cross
Robe and crown
Large wall map of your county
Prerecorded ceremonial music.
Pocket New Testament
Club, gun, and handcuffs
Tote bag full of Bibles
Hat or cap with protective cushion in it

Performance Tips

For stronger impact, insert the name of local places (cities, counties, rivers, etc.) wherever indicated.

Use lights to signal scene changes.

Instead of performing the TV show live onstage, you may choose to videotape the entire program beforehand and play it on the TV at the appropriate time. Unless you use a large-screen TV however, your audience would probably have difficulty seeing and hearing the program.

You may also choose to build a giant TV screen frame to sit in front of the TV setting to help the audience understand that the family is watching this program on TV.

Scene One: *opens on living room side with Sue reading the* TV Guide *and Gary reading the newspaper, each seated in chairs or on couch as lights come on.*

Sue (*scans* TV Guide *as she speaks*): How should we celebrate the Fourth of July? (*Pauses, points to magazine*): Here's a program that looks like a good one—on XYZ. (*Checks watch*): It starts in two minutes. (*Picks up remote control, gestures toward other side of stage.*) (Optional line): A perfect show for our new, big-screen TV.

Gary (*glances at watch, then back to newspaper*): Just so it doesn't last more than five minutes.

Sue (*surprised*): Did you have something else planned?

Gary (*eyes still on the newspaper*): Of course; the (   ) game.

Sue: But you'll love this program! (*Reads excitedly*): "As a special Fourth of July extravaganza, XYZ will introduce two new television inventions: Spirit Contact and Pretendo. Each is an amazing technological discovery. The Spirit Contact equipment permits interviews with persons in Heaven!" (*Looks up*): That's fantastic! (*Quickly back to* TV Guide): "And Pretendo technology allows us to change history. Used together, the viewers will be able to participate in the most exciting and educational July Fourth celebration ever!"

Gary (*looks at watch*): Now you've got three minutes.

Sue (*continues reading aloud*): "The guests from the spirit world will be George Washington, John Quincy Adams, and Thomas Paine. Each of these men played a vital role in the early history of our nation." (*Looks at Gary, then goes back to* *reading silently*): Hey! This says that part of the program will take place right here in (city)! This is a show we shouldn't miss—it's a television first!

Gary: I don't care. I've been waiting all week for this game.

Sue (*exasperated*): Oh, Gary! You can watch a ball game any day. (*Reads aloud from* TV *Guide*): "The purpose of this program is to provide a deeper appreciation of our many freedoms on this, our nation's birthday."

Gary: But who wants to watch a boring, old program on history? I had enough of that in high school.

Sue (*pleading*): It lasts only thirty minutes.

Gary: But the pregame show starts in two minutes! Look, the only way to celebrate the Fourth is to watch a baseball game—that's the all-American pastime! Besides, a game will get our minds off our problems—that other show won't!

Sue: You sure are grouchy today.

Gary: All they'll talk about is how wonderful it is living in America. Nonsense! We all know better than that; the crime rate gets worse everyday, we have rotten politicians, sky-high income taxes, runaway inflation, and the country's a polluted mess; life here can't get much worse!

Sue: Let's watch it for ten minutes. Then if you don't like it, we'll switch to the pregame interviews. Okay?

Gary (*angrily*): OK, but just for ten minutes and that's it! (*Grabs newspaper, continues reading When Sue turns on the* TV, *they both watch intently, reacting appropriately throughout.*)

End of Scene One

Scene Two: *When Sue directs the remote at the* TV *and pushes the button, the lights come up on Alan, George, John and Thomas as they are entering the* TV *studio and taking their seats.*

Alan: This is Alan Griffin for XYZ, with a history-making program demonstrating for the first time ever, our new **Spirit Contact** and **Pretendo** equipment. With these amazing new inventions, we are able to visit with (*gestures to each*): George Washington, John Quincy Adams, and Thomas Paine. (*Each nods as name is called.*) Thank you for coming—ah, for being with us today. I'll try keep the interview short so that you won't miss your Thanksgiving worship service in Heaven.

I understand that in Heaven, you are able to monitor all activity that takes place here on earth; do you have any comments regarding the activity of Americans today with regard to Independence Day?

George (*nods*): Yes, I do. I'm greatly concerned about the widespread apathy prevailing in the United States of America. It's almost like U.S. citizens don't know, or value, the freedoms they enjoy. (*Lifts a notebook*): I got these notes from our Statistics Department—as you know, we have access to all knowledge in Heaven. (*Reads from notes*): Yesterday, the ratio of prayers of gratitude to prayers of request from those living in the United States was only two out of every thousand prayers. This ratio has experienced a steady decline ever since we founded this country—except for small peaks every time there's a war anywhere in the world.

Thomas (*nods*): I'm sorry to say "I told you so," but I saw this coming over two hundred years ago. As I said in one speech, "What we obtain too cheaply, we esteem too lightly." Since you (*gestures toward audience*) Americans living today have made no personal sacrifice to maintain your liberty, it's extremely difficult—if not impossible—to *really* appreciate the freedoms you have.

John: These freedoms, or rights, that you take so lightly are the direct result of our (*gestures to the others*) deep, religious convictions. That's affirmed in the Declaration of Independence. It states that all people "are endowed by their Creator with certain inalienable rights." And yet on this day set aside to commemorate our nation's birth, only two out of every thousand people who prayed thanked God for living in this country! The rest complained, or simply took the nation for granted by not praying for it at all.

Alan: Research by XYZ supports those statistics. Now the question is, what can we do about the general apathy?

Thomas: Before you contacted us last week to appear on this show, we had already heard about both of these new inventions. As we discussed your invitation, George had a great idea for the PRETENDO technology.

George: Yes. I thought looking at the way things might have been could have a real impact on citizens of the U.S. today.

I suggested we change some facts preceding the American Revolution using PRETENDO technology. By rewriting history, we can see the tragedy that might have been.

Alan (*excitedly*): And the XYZ board of directors approved your proposal! Before today's show, we tested the PRETENDO equipment on several past elections and one World Series game. We simply fed different facts into our computer and ran the program. The results were amazing!

George: We hope the audience will understand that we're not actually changing history, but observing what might have happened if circumstances had been a little different.

John: Shall we begin? These will be facts that might very well have been true. (*Looks up, thinking, then programs each fact on a remote control*): First of all, let's assume our founders had no religious convictions whatsoever; they were non-believers across-the-board. Secondly, let's suppose they were controlled entirely by distrust, hatred, lust for power, and greed. Thirdly, we'll assume that Christianity didn't arrive in this country until around 1870—and then only in certain areas. Finally, as a direct result of the foregoing facts, the Declaration of Independence, the Constitution, and the Bill of Rights were never written. Which means the United States of America was never formed. (*To Thomas and George*): Do you have any other PRETENDO facts we should plug in?

George (*hesitates*): Well, how about these? (*As he speaks, John programs.*) Similar to many countries in the world today, terrorism, civil war, and anarchy have prevailed for more than two hundred years. Because of that, this country has been divided into separate nations, most of them ruled by dictators—just like we find in many parts of the world today.

Thomas: To simplify this presentation, let's focus upon one specific geographical area. Let's use (your city and state).

John (*displays remote to audience*): When I press this button, the PRETENDO computer will take over the televised program. Please bear with us should there be any transmission delay. (*Raises remote control, presses button. Lights go off the TV studio.*)

As quickly as possible, the four men leave the TV set and the general enters. To camouflage their scurrying around, Sue and Gary exclaim, "What's happening? Is there something wrong with our set?," etc. As soon as the general and the map of your county are in place, the lights come back up on the TV studio.

General: Ladies and Gentlemen! Welcome to "The State of Perfection." Our Holy dictator is Frederick the Perfect and I'm his top general. (*Gestures to auditorium*): This is the public room of the holy castle. For all you tourists here today, I'll describe Perfection. (*Points to map of your county. Names of local places have been changed*) We live here in Frederickville, named after our fearless leader. These other communities (*points to places on map*): were named after the children of our great leader; Anna, Michael, Karen, Theodore, and Joseph (*points to communities on the map*). Due to the wars that have been fought since the settlement of this continent for the past two hundred years, our boundaries are constantly changing, but Frederick the Perfect has a new map drawn for himself monthly, and these *are* the current boundaries.

Woman #1 in audience raises her hand, the general recognizes her.

Woman #1: I'm from Canada. I'm on my way to take a gift to my uncle, who lives on the west side of uh, Perfection.

General (*peers out into the audience, says in shock*): Is that a *cross* you're wearing around your neck? If you value your life, don't let our Holy Dictator see that! He'll be entering the room at any moment!

Woman #1: Why should I hide it? In Canada, we have the right to wear symbols of our religious belief. I'm not afraid to let the world know that I'm a Christian!

General (*getting frantic*): Don't *ever* use that word—that "C" word—in the presence of our leader!! That's a federal crime! (*Moves his finger quickly across his throat*): Your head will roll! (*Pause.*) Now, to get back to my presentation. . . .

Woman #1: Wait a minute! You can't tell me not to wear religious symbols and not to talk about my faith! Those are my rights as a citizen! Just like I have freedom of speech, and the press has freedom, and—

General (*puzzled*): What's a press?

Woman #1: T*he* press! It's the mass media industry—you know, newspapers, magazines, radio, television—

General (*interrupting, very upset*): His Holy Majesty has banned all such subversive activity! Distributing information to the masses will get you killed in this country! Now please, madam, let me get back to my introduction! Military training starts at age eleven for both males and females. They begin fighting at twelve. Since they're shorter than adults, they make smaller targets for enemy guns. Military expenses make up 85 percent of our national budget.

Woman #1: In Canada, our largest expense is human services: 79 percent of *our* budget provides free health care, including a hospital for each community. Our government and churches provide food and clothes for the needy.

General (*ignoring her, but clearly agitated*): The other 15 percent goes to support our holy leader, his four wives, fifteen children, twelve slaves, fifty servants, and seventy-five personal security guards, as well as the security fence that surrounds his estate in (name of local public park).

Woman #1 (*persistent*): I don't understand; what's left of the national budget to support the public schools in Perfection?

General (*puzzled*): What do you mean—"public schools?"

Woman #1: Government-funded schools for all children.

General (*laughs*): Who ever heard of such a thing? Once upon a time we did have some do-gooders who proposed schools funded with private money, but it was a total flop! In Perfection, the economic fact is, as soon as kids learn to walk, they learn to work. And later, to fight for our holy dictator. We can't permit literacy among the general public; education *always* produces subversive factions!

Woman #1 (*snorts in derision*): Well, are there any paved roads in this country?

General (*shakes head*): We don't need any. We travel on foot or on horseback. We have only two roads—both are old, dirt-surfaced Indian trails.

Woman #1 (*chuckles*): I found that out the hard way! I started over here in a rainstorm, but had to stop when I came to the border of Perfection. Your Indian trails were knee-deep in mud. I had to leave my van at the border.

General (*puzzled*): What's a van?

Woman #1: It's a vehicle for transporting people.

General: Vehicle? You mean like some kind of wagon?

Woman #1: Oh, no. It's bigger than a station wagon. A van is sort of like an enclosed truck with seats for many passengers. . . . There's really no way I can explain it.

General (*agitated*): What good is a stationary wagon?! And what is a truck?! Back to my introduction! Frederick the Perfect is also our religious leader, appointed by God to rule this area. He tolerates no religion other than the religion of the National Temple, of which he is the head. When he enters, you must rise and humbly bow. You are not permitted to look upon his face until he is seated. After the meeting, he will answer a few questions. Raise your hand and when he recognizes you, stand, bow, and ask your question.

Play prerecorded ceremonial music.

General: Here comes Frederick the Perfect! (*Gestures*): Please stand and bow until he is seated.

As Frederick and servant enter, General bows, and remains in that position until Frederick is seated. Servant kneels at Frederick's feet as music fades and stops. General returns to standing position.

General (*motions to audience*): Please be seated.

Fred the P (*angrily snaps fingers*): Servant! Where's my coffee?

Servant dashes to table, pours coffee, returns to Frederick, kneels.

Fred the P (*angrily*): And where's my napkin?

Servant (*still kneeling, bows head to Frederick's feet*): I beg your mercy, Your Holy Majesty. it was a terrible mistake. Please spare my life. (*Quickly stands, dashes to table, returns with napkin, kneels before Frederick, hands him napkin.*)

Fred the P: The next time, don't forget it! (*To General*): Give me the latest battle report.

General (*bows*): Your Holy Majesty, sixty-five of your royal troops are known dead, 143 still missing in action.

Fred the P: And how many enemy soldiers were killed?

General: We estimated eighty-three killed.

Fred the P: Were there any prisoners?

General: We took twenty-three. They were immediately shot.

Fred the P: Good! That cuts expenses. How many draftees are needed for tomorrow's battle along the (local) River?

General: At least seventy-five. And we don't have time to train them.

Fred the P (*stands*): Everybody here (*gestures around room*) is ordered to report to headquarters immediately after this meeting. Bring enough food for three days. No meals are served on the front. (*Sits down.*) Now for the financial report.

General: Our defense spending went sky-high this month, higher than income. To cut back, we're converting our only medical shack into barracks for new draftees. Also, the soldiers are now being paid in clothes and blankets only—no cash or food. Except for your royal officers, of course. They still receive warm food three times a day prepared and served by your royal servants.

Fred the P: Good! Now for the anti-religion report.

General (*smiles proudly*): We just had our best month on record! We picked up reports about a person named Smith who was trafficking in Bibles. We demolished seventy-eight Smith residences in surprise searches before we found the right house on (   ) Avenue. We burned twenty-four Bibles but the owners refused to tell us the name of their supplier, so we sentenced the thirteen children to hard labor for life. The ten adults were immediately executed.

Fred the P (*broad smile*): Good job, General!

General: We also uncovered a group of "believers." They called themselves the "(local) Church." Before we executed them, each admitted knowing the law—no unlicensed religious services. Except yours, of course. We also found a Bible at the house of one of your staff members. What shall we do with him, his wife, and two babies?

Fred the P (*finger across throat*): Or better yet, torture the adults until they break. We *must* find the name of that Bible supplier! After they spill their guts, chop off their heads!

General (*studies notes*): We've got a problem, Your Holiness; we can't execute them until next Thursday.

Fred the P (*angrily*): When I order it, do it! Immediately!

General: But Your Majesty, the royal guillotine needs to be repaired—it's been overused. The blade's shot.

Fred the P: OK, get a new one ASAP! Any more business?

General (*looks at notes*): One suspect wasn't home last night when we made the Bible raids, but I think I spotted him out there! (*Looks at audience, points*): That's him! You! Stand up!

Man #1 (*stands, bows*): What have I done?

General: That's what I'm going to find out! That bulge in your coat pocket—what is it?

Man #1 (*pulls it out*): It's called a pocket New Testament—a friend gave it to me.

General (*runs to man, grabs* Testament, *yells to* Fred): What shall I do with him?

Fred the P: The same as those other Bible-readers. First, torture him to find out who gave him the illegal book. Then, (*finger across throat*) zap! That's your job, General, to put a stop to this exploding crime wave!

General (*handcuffs the man, sends him backstage, turns, speaks to audience*): His Holy Majesty will now answer questions.

Woman #1 raises her hand.

Fred the P: State your question.

Woman #1 (*stands, bows*): Your Holy Majesty, do you permit women to work at government jobs?

Fred the P (*shakes head*): A woman's place is to bear children, preferably males—and lots of them. At twelve, they're mean and make great fighters. Childless women are either drafted into the army, or become servants in the royal castle.

Woman #1: In Canada, where I'm from, women are permitted to hold any jobs for which they are qualified.

Fred the P (*to General*): After this meeting, search her! Then give her a flogging—thirty stripes on the back. We don't need this kind of trouble-maker in Perfection!

Woman #1 sits down. Woman #2 raises her hand.

Fred the P (*to woman*): Yes?

Woman #2 (*stands, bows, grieving*): Your Holy Majesty, our daughter and son were killed in the (local) massacre. They were only twelve and thirteen. May we remove their bodies from the battlefield?

Fred the P: Absolutely not! You know the rules: all battle zones are restricted areas—military personnel only!

Woman #2: But they deserve a decent burial!

Fred the P (*to General*): Arrest that woman! Give her five years of hard labor!

General dashes to woman, handcuffs her, sends her backstage. Man in following dialogue should wear hat or cap with small piece of metal for sound impact and protective cushion beneath. Man #2 raises hand.

Fred the P (*sees man*): Yes?

Man #2 (*stands, bows*): Your Holy Majesty, I ran a fishing business along the (local) River. Last month, your navy placed mines in that area. I lost both my boats and all my crew members. Now I'm out of a job and my wife and children are starving. Will I be repaid for those lost boats?

Fred the P: Absolutely not! Where's your patriotism? Think of all our soldiers who gave their lives for the royal family!

Man #2 (*angrily*): Well, what about paying for my dock? They cut it up for firewood!

Fred the P: No way! Same reason.

Man #2: What about the wagons and horses they stole? And our house—three soldiers moved right in and forced us to provide them with room and board!

Fred the P (*to General*): I thought you screened this group!! (*Turns back to man*): What are you—an agitator? (*Jabs finger at him.*) You do what I say! I ordered the navy to secure all waterways from all possible invaders! It's that simple! And to answer your other questions, it's your patriotic duty to supply the military with whatever they need! If I hear one more smart remark from you, I'll—

Man #2 (*shakes fist*): Don't we have any rights at all?

Fred the P: Arrest that agitator! He gets life in prison!

General dashes toward man.

Man #2: But in other countries, the government is not permitted to take property without reimbursement, or imprison people without public jury trials!

Fred the P (*to General*): Club him! Then off with his head! (*Finger across throat.*)

General pulls out club, knocks man to floor, picks him up, sends him offstage as Fred *is speaking.*

Fred the P (*sees* Woman #3 *raise her hand*): Yes?

Woman #3 (*stands, bows*): Your Holy Majesty, I've been your slave my entire life because of my English blood. My mother recently died and my father married a woman of German descent. Am I entitled to citizenship here in Perfection?

Fred the P (*shakes head*): Nope! Once a slave, always a slave! You're stuck with it. Besides, how do you expect me to run the castle without slaves? Just be thankful you're alive.

Woman #3 sits down. Man #3 raises his hand.

Fred the P (*sees raised hand*): Yes?

Man #3 (*stands, bows*): Your Majesty, I'm worried about the total lack of medical care for our injured soldiers at the front. Is there some way we can get help to them? They're dying by the hundreds. Couldn't the government at least hire a doctor and some nurses from another country?

Fred the P (*to General*): Arrest that man! Give him ten years for criticizing my policy!!

General dashes toward man.

Man #3 (*fist outstretched*): I demand a trial by jury! And a lawyer!

Fred the P: Who do you think you are, God? (*To General*): Make that life in prison!

General grabs man, handcuffs him, sends him offstage.

Man #3 (*shouting*): I've read where some countries allow citizens freedom of speech!

Fred the P (*furious, turns to General*): Shoot him!

General draws pistol, shoots him. Man grabs stomach, staggers.

Fred the P (*to General*): Get him out of here quickly so all that blood won't mess up the royal carpet!

General runs man offstage as Frederick *speaks.*

Fred the P (*points to woman #1*): You! What's that hanging around your neck?

Woman #1 (*touches it*): It's a cross, Your Majesty.

Fred the P: You dare wear a cross in this country? That's blasphemy! (*To General*): Search that bag in her hand!

General (*dashes to her, opens bag. To Frederick*): It's filled with Bibles, Your Holy Majesty!

Fred the P: So! *She's* the Bible-runner! What's your name?

Woman #1: Vivian Smith.

Fred the P (*leaps from chair*): Smith! That's the Smith we've been searching for! Shoot her!

General pulls out gun and shoots her. Woman #1 doubles over, falls to floor. General helps her to her feet, then quickly rushes her offstage.

Fred the P: Bible-runners are dangerous! They rank right up there with the world's worst terrorists! That makes this the biggest crime bust in the history of Perfection! I'm going to declare this a national holiday! (*Checks watch*): Now it's time for you to declare your allegiance for me.

General and Servant (*drop to knees, bow heads, clasp hands in front of face*): We worship only you, Frederick the Perfect. You saved our country from demons of democracy and false religions. To you, we give our lives and property—forever.

Recorded ceremonial music plays. General and servant stand. Frederick leads procession from the stage with General and servant following. Music stops. Lights go off. Alan, George, John, and Thomas return to their original positions in chairs. Lights come back on.

Alan (*excitedly*): That was the most amazing program I've ever seen! The tragic results of dictatorship—the beatings and shootings—are happening today all around the world. They could just as easily be happening all across our country—a truly frightening thought! I'm sure our audience will be interested in learning your reactions.

George: After seeing that, I'm even more convinced that our faith and trust in God made the difference. Without His guidance, you (*gestures to audience*) could be living under tyrannical conditions.

John: George once spoke about the importance of trusting God at all times and being grateful for His benefits. That's what it takes to face *all* of our problems—large and small.

Thomas (*nods*): That same trust in God became the solid foundation of our entire legal system. That's what made our country unique among all nations.

Alan (*to Washington*): What's your reaction to that?

George (*nods*): I totally agree. Our Declaration of Independence, which we signed on July 4, 1776, reflects that deeply-felt trust in the statement, "With a firm reliance on the protection of the Divine Providence, we mutually pledge to each other our lives, our fortunes, and our sacred honor."

Alan: What impact did the Bible have on your personal lives?

Thomas (*glances at Adams*): John gave us the best example; "The first and almost the only Book deserving of universal attention is the Bible." Do you remember that, John?

John: I'll never forget it. It's the central thread in our Constitution. And Noah Webster agreed completely. He once said, "All the miseries and evils which men suffer from vice, crime, ambition, injustice, oppression, slavery, and war proceed from their despising or neglecting the precepts of the Bible."

Thomas (*briefly glances at George*): When George was chairing the Constitutional Convention, he stopped a heated argument by pleading, "Let us raise a standard to which the wise and the honest can repair. The event is now in the hands of God."

Alan (*to George*): What was your reaction when the Constitution was finally enacted?

George: I felt like celebrating a victory! God had guided us through many sessions. The harmony between the strongest of opposing forces was like a miracle.

John: Our faith made the difference. A few years after George became president, he stated, "It is the duty of all nations to acknowledge the providence of Almighty God, to obey His will, to be grateful for His benefits, and to humbly implore His protection and favor."

Alan (*to George*): What was your reaction to the Bill of Rights?

George: It was a dream come true. Back when the Constitution was first signed, I made a prediction that was partially fulfilled by the Bill of Rights. You see, the Constitution was a compromise agreement. I recognized that it was the best we could achieve, given who we were—

mere mortals—and the time we lived in. But we would work toward making it a more perfect instrument of liberty and justice for all. And that's what happened in the Bill of Rights and later amendments. The Constitution is still not perfect, but your leaders are still trying to improve it.

Alan (*to Thomas*): What was your reaction to the Bill of Rights?

Thomas: I thought it was long overdue. I see God's hand in each freedom: religion, speech, and press. And since there is no perfect way to determine guilt, a public trial is the best system around anywhere. That PRETENDO simulation showed the clear result when we violate the teachings of Christ. Each of you (*gestures toward audience*) is protected by the Bill of Rights from all those terrible tragedies we just witnessed.

Alan: Mr. Adams, what was your reaction to the Bill of Rights?

John: The first ten ammendments to the Constitution were the best improvements we could possibly have made. PRETENDO showed us the tragedies that are happening around the world in countries where citizens have few or no rights. For example, searching houses without court orders, punishing suspects, even killing them on the spot, without trials. And torturing prisoners seldom fails to get confessions—whether the confession is true or false.

Thomas: The man who lost his possesions would have been reimbursed by the government of the United States. And this idea of fairness comes straight from the Bible; Do unto others as you would have them do unto you.

George: Another important right is freedom of religion. That was a unique concept back when we formed the foundations for this country. In Perfection, worshiping the God of your choice was the worst crime on the books. To a dictator, Christians are the most dangerous criminals of all since they worship and follow a different leader. The message of love is considered subversive.

Alan: I've always assumed citizens of the United States had that right even before the Bill was passed.

George: Not at all. Religious freedom was a completely new idea in the world at that time. Back in my day, Virginia permitted only one religion. Back in 1620, 167 years before our Constitution, England had a similar law that permitted only one denomination—the Church of England. That is why, after many years of persecution by the English government, the Puritans fled from their country. They gave up all they had to come to this continent. Their deep beliefs contributed to that First Amendment many years later.

John: That same Christian belief in the dignity of individuals appears in our Declaration of Independence. It begins with, "We, the people . . . ." Power starts with the people, not with government officials. The later amendments gave women and Afro-Americans the same rights as the rest of us. Putting people first is a concept found first in the Bible.

Alan: And today, that "people first" concept is sweeping the world.

John (*nods*): It's exploding. Enslaved citizens of many countries have seen the results of the rights found in the United States, including the freedoms we fought and died for in the 1700's. The same ones you (*gestures to audience*) enjoy today. The PRETENDO simulation showed us the kind of life-and-death existence faced by those living under dictators around the world.

George (*gestures to audience*): You have been blessed just by being born, or by living here. You did nothing to deserve it—put forth no effort, no risk of life. If you are irritated by the exploding crime rate, politicians, taxes, or inflation, think about what your life could be like elsewhere. You could move to any number of countries where you would not have the freedom you have here. If you did, either you or a close friend could be tortured unmercifully or simply executed on the spot, just as we saw in Perfection.

Alan: Thank you very much. You have helped us better understand what it means to live in America. Our freedoms are the result of God acting through you and others—gifts we didn't earn. (*To audience*): Without our early Christian leaders, we would not have the many blessings and opportunities we have today. We can be thankful for those selfless people who gave their all—even their lives—for us. The United States of America began with these (*gestures toward the three guests*) and many other dedicated Christians who took a stand against tyranny. May we continue to look to God for leadership and support. Good night from XYZ Network.

END OF SCENE TWO

Scene Three: *Sue and Gary sit with bowed heads.*

Sue (*shakes head*): I never realized what it meant to be born here. Being born in a free country was something we had no control over. (*Pauses.*) We could just as easily have been born in Lebanon, or Iraq, or, anyplace!

Gary (*shakes head*): And all I've done is complain about this country. (*Pauses.*) It's gonna take me some time to sort this out. (*Pause.*) Just think; the deep Christian convictions of our founding fathers have had a profound impact upon our lives. (*Head bowed, hand to forehead.*)

Sue: If it hadn't been for their persistent, dedicated faith and hope, we could be living in a country like that one called "Perfection."

Gary (*shakes head*): I can't imagine what it would be like to live under such conditions! To have no rights or freedoms of any kind? How can those poor people exist from day to day?

Sue: I'm deeply grateful for our founders—their hope and faith in God made freedom possible for us. We are truly blessed. (*Pauses.*) We would probably have been killed in battle at age twelve.

Gary (*looks up, excitedly*): And we would never have met, fallen in love, and gotten married! Thank God for the faith of the men who founded this country, and for the freedom we enjoy! (*Gary and Sue embrace and kiss.*)

Curtain

The Bottom Line

Characters

Robert Nicholson; father, greedy, snobbish businessman, city council member, age 50's
Barbara Nicholson; mother, loving homemaker, age 50's
Janet Nicholson; daughter, concerned college student
Theresa Neumann; TV news anchorperson, age 30-45
Doug Orwell; fire fighter, forgiving, age 25-40
Kevin Watkins; fire fighter, strong-willed, age 25-40
Two voices; recorded for playback, or performed live offstage

Scenes

Scene 1: Basement family room/TV set
Scene 2: Hospital recovery room/TV set

Performance Tips

Entire play is performed on a split stage. On one side is a basement family room which will become a hospital room in scene two, the other side is a TV set (where shows are performed live, onstage).

You may choose to pre-film both TV interviews for showing on an actual TV, however, it is doubtful that your audience would be able to see and hear these. You may also choose to build a frame to simulate a TV screen. This would "house" the actors/actresses during the TV interviews. Whichever option is used, angle the TV set slightly toward the other side as if actors/actresses, as well as the audience, are watching it. During interviews, characters are seated, behind a table.

Use lights to signal scene changes.

Props

Beside whatever props you decide to have for your settings, you will need:

Seats for three in the family room, magazine, telephone

A remote control (in both scenes), VCR and tape on stand

Taped telephone conversations (Unless you decide to perform them live.)

Taped sound effects (Check with your local library.)

Fire fighter's hat, coat, fire extinguisher
Notes for TV interview
Bed, pillows, blanket, hospital gown, bandages
Signs: CHANNEL 9, and ROOM 3A-49

Scene One: *Robert Nicholson is sitting in his family room, impatiently scanning a magazine when the phone rings.*

Recorded sound *of telephone ringing.*

Robert (*picks up receiver, answers*): Bob Nicholson speaking.

Ed's recorded voice: Hi, Bob. This is Ed down at the store. I thought you should know what just happened. Some guy from the Fire Department was snooping around your storage building out back.

Robert: What was he looking for?

Ed: He asked if you still stored naphtha and lacquer in there. So I took him inside—and of course he didn't find one container! I told him you took your city council obligations seriously—that you'd never violate that new law about storing dangerous substances! He thanked me and left.

Robert: That's right! I'd never commit a crime—unless forced to! (*Both explode into laughter.*) I'm just glad we moved all that stuff into my garage before they checked out the store.

Ed: It was perfect timing! They'll never catch on.

Robert: Oh, I hear Janet and Barb upstairs—Janet must be home from school. I'll have to hang up. (*Hangs up. Janet and Barbara enter, Janet goes to Robert, hugs him.*)

Janet: Hi, Dad! It's good to see you! I haven't seen you since last May—every time I come home, you're at work or at a council meeting. (*They sit down.*)

Robert: You know how it is—work comes first. Otherwise, we'd starve. (*Grins*): And you'd have to drop out of school. Are you home for a while?

Janet: Yes. Now that the quarter is over, I can take a break.

Barbara: I'm *relieved* to have you home! After that fire in your dorm last week, I'm not sure that I want you to go back! We saw it on the evening news—(*she shudders*) smoke pouring out of the top, flames lighting up the sky for miles around. I just knew you'd been killed in the explosion!

Robert: We were certainly glad when you called.

Janet: I thank God no one was killed. It could have been a total disaster.

Robert: Where were you when the fire broke out?

Janet: In my room, getting ready for bed. Immediately after the explosion, I felt the floor shake. The entire dorm was shocked into silence for a few seconds, then the screaming in the hallway started. I dashed out and found two girls frozen with fear—completely unable to move. Three others kept running around in circles, screaming.

Robert (*shakes his head*): What did you do then?

Janet: I was desperate—and scared! I sent up a prayer for help, then I saw smoke rolling down the hallway. I calmed down the two frozen statues and led them to the exit. Then I ran back and directed some more girls out to safety.

Barbara: Were any of the students on your floor injured?

Janet (*shakes head*): No, they all made it out okay. But three students on the third floor were badly burned. They won't be released from the hospital for several weeks.

Barbara: Did they ever find out what caused the explosion?

Janet (*nods*): It started in a storage room on the third floor. The maintenance crew had stored lacquer and naphtha there, and cleaning rags. The fire investigators later found a short in the wiring. That's what must have ignited the fumes from the lacquer and naphtha containers.

Barbara: I didn't realize how dangerous that stuff could be.

Janet (*nods*): In fact, those substances are so dangerous, the city just recently passed a new law requiring special protective storage procedures. I understand the prosecutor is considering filing criminal charges against the university.

Barbara: Well, he should! That was a serious violation!

Janet: After reading the newspaper reports, I realized just how close we all came to being killed. If it hadn't been for those dedicated fire fighters, the students on the upper floors would have been killed in that second explosion.

Barbara: Thank God it wasn't any worse.

Janet (*looks toward* Robert, *puzzled*): Dad, I noticed you've filled the garage with storage containers.

Robert (*uncomfortable*): Yes, I needed a place to hold our supplies from the store.

Janet (*amazed*): It's so full, there's no room for your car. What's in all those containers?

Robert (*hesitates, tries evasion*): Oh, ah . . . different things.

Janet: I don't understand. What kind of things?

Robert (*shrugs*): Just some supplies we couldn't store at work.

Janet: Like what?

Robert (*reluctant*): Oh, a few containers of naphtha and lacquer.

Barbara (*totally shocked*): Robert! That's what caused those explosions at school! That stuff is dangerous!

Robert (*shakes head, waves hand*): Don't worry about it, Barbara. It'll be okay.

Barbara: But storing it in unapproved buildings is against the law! What if someone reports you? You could go to jail!

Robert (*winks at Barbara*): Not to worry. That's one of the hidden benefits of my being a member of the city council. Besides, I saved more than two thousand dollars!

Janet: I don't understand!

Throughout Robert's explanation, both women react appropriately, puzzled, upset, angry.

Robert: That new storage law is just another way to soak the businessman! It requires expensive containers, structures, and detection devices for storing all flammable materials. It would cost me $2500 or more to build the kind of shed they want—and that's absolutely ridiculous! (*Grins smugly.*) So I built some shelves in the garage and wired it for lighting. And it only cost $400 in materials! It doesn't take a college degree to do a little carpentry, you know!

Barbara (*angrily*): You wired it yourself? You're not licensed to do that, are you? (*Turns to Janet*): Didn't you say a short in the wiring caused that explosion at school?

Robert (*shakes head, waves hand*): You worry too much, Barbara. I'm just being practical—saving the company money. Those crazy laws are just to make laborers and contractors rich.

Janet (*shocked*): I can't believe what I'm hearing! You'd risk both your life and Mom's just to save some money?

Robert: That's my job, Jan, to make a profit for the company. And there's no simpler way to make a profit than by cutting expenses. When I need construction work done at the store; I just hire students from the vocational school at minimum wage. I refuse to pay those ridiculous union wages for work that any ten-year-old could do.

Janet: I don't understand you, Dad! Here we are, celebrating Labor Day, and at the same time, you're figuring out ways to cheat honest laborers!

Robert (*angry*): I'm not cheating anyone! If I can hire my work done at less than union wages, I make a bigger profit! And that's the bottom line. That's how I keep food on our table, *and you* in school so that you can have a *good* career!

Janet (*hesitates, speaks slowly to* Robert): Speaking of careers, I've got something very important to tell you, Dad. I just hope I can find the right words to explain it to you.

Robert (*puzzled*): What are you talking about?

Janet (*hesitates, then*): For the past several months, I've been doing some serious soul-searching about my future—trying to decide what I should do.

Robert: That's easy—stick with your business courses so you can take over the company when I retire.

Janet (*nods*): I know that's always been our plan, Dad, and I appreciate your offer. None of my friends at school have a career guaranteed like that. But ever since that summer in high school when I worked for you, I haven't felt sure that I'm suited for business. Now, after two years of business courses, I'm convinced that I'm not.

Robert (*explodes*): How can you do that to me? Two years of college—totally wasted!

Barbara (*to* Robert): That's not fair to her, Bob. Listen to what she has to say. (*To* Janet): Have you made any decisions as to what you do want to do with your life?

Janet (*nods*): I've always wanted to help people on a one-to-one basis. But I wasn't sure exactly how to do that—until that fire in the dorm. I saw very clearly how well I handled that emergency; I was one of a few students whose mind worked at all. The fire was a real test of my faith and skills—and I found them both to be strong. After praying about it for several days, I made my decision. I want to drop out of college and enroll in the vocational school; I want to get into fire prevention and safety.

Robert (*shocked*): Do you mean . . . be a fire fighter?

Janet (*nods*): That's right.

Robert (*bitterly angry*): And throw away your entire future?

Janet: The way I see it, I'll have a terrific future. I'll be matching my skills with an important community service, and learning how to save people from serious injury and death. Living to serve others is straight out of the Bible—"the real bottom line," to quote a phrase you often use.

Robert (*bitterly*): You always did take the Bible too seriously!

Janet (*shakes head*): That's not possible, Dad.

Robert: But I thought you wanted an important job!

Janet: Fire fighting is important! It means saving lives as well as property!

Robert (*shakes head angrily*): You just don't understand the real world out there! Take it from me—I've got more than thirty years of experience; you've got to go for the big bucks—that's where the real action—

Recorded sound *of telephone ringing.*

Robert (*jumps, turns to* Barbara): I'll take that call in the other room. Get out that video of last month's interview and show it to her (*points to* TV/*set*): on our new, big-screen TV. Maybe that'll help her understand the *real* facts of life. I'll be right back. (H*e leaves.* M*ake sure phone rings throughout speech.*)

Barbara: Your father has some very strong opinions I hope you won't take his outburst too personally.

Janet: Sometimes he's difficult, Mom—very difficult. He has no idea how important certain workers are to all of us. (P*ause.*) I just hope that he'll see how much it means to me to be able to help other people in a personal way.

Barbara picks up video tape and inserts into the VCR. W*hile she is* *doing this, Robert, Doug, and Theresa enter TV side of stage and sit at table, Theresa in the center chair. Barbara holds up remote control, presses a button and lights come up on the TV scene.*

Theresa: I'm Theresa Neumann for Channel 9 News, reporting on the results of tonight's City Council meeting. With me are Robert Nicholson, council member, and Doug Orwell, (city) Fire Chief. (*Each nod as his name is called. To Doug*): Would you explain that proposal you made on behalf of the department?

Doug (*nods*): We're deeply concerned about the disastrous explosions and fires caused by hazardous substances around the country. In our city, we have neither the equipment, the training, nor the personnel to effectively fight chemical fires. Currently, there is no way to enforce the new law recently passed by our state legislature that sets standards for the storing of dangerous materials. We studied the new law, met with fire fighters across the state, and analyzed our own particular problems in this community. We came up with four proposals to submit to council.

Theresa: Would you describe them for us?

Doug: Certainly. (*Reads from note*): First, we need a disaster squad specifically trained to fight chemical fires; then we will need special protective gear. Thirdly, we propose hiring a part-time investigator; and lastly, we are asking for a 3 percent wage increase for department employees.

Theresa: Would you explain the purpose of an investigator?

Doug: The experience of other counties in the state is that many businesses regularly and intentionally violate the fire safety codes as a way of avoiding the financial costs of implementing the new legal requirements for storing hazardous substances. After checking businesses around town, we are convinced that the same violations are occurring here in our own community. Business owners are storing dangerous substances in sheds and garages that do not meet the requirements of the new law. We desperately need a licensed, investigative officer.

Robert: Are you suggesting people are violating the law?

Doug: It's not just a suggestion, Mr. Nicholson. It's a fact. Many businesses are intentionally committing criminal acts by concealing their explosive materials in unsafe places.

Robert (*angrily*): It sounds to me like you're basing your allegations on mere gossip. Can you prove any of this?

Doug: We are so undermanned, we don't have anyone with the time and skills to properly investigate. That's why we need to create a new position.

Robert: But we haven't had a serious fire here in more than twelve years.

Doug (*calmly*): But that doesn't mean we won't. Over the past decade, the variety and quantity of dangerous substances has doubled throughout our state. Just last year in ( ) County, a chemical tanker explosion destroyed six houses and two commercial buildings, and killed eight people. One of those killed was a fireman with inadequate gear and training for such a disaster.

Robert: But that happened clear over in ( ) County!

Doug (*points to floor*): It could just as easily have occurred right here in ( ). Disaster training would prepare us for such catastrophes. That translates into better prevention and safety throughout our entire community.

Robert (*irritated*): Have you given any consideration to the tremendous financial impact this new storage law has had on our local business owners?

Doug (*nods*): Yes, we have. And we've compared that cost with the tragic loss of life and permanent injuries sustained in chemical disasters. Which is more important, Mr. Nicholson: business profits, or lives and permanent injuries?

Robert (*bitterly*): I assume that the request for a 3 percent raise was for community safety, too?

Doug (*aggravated*): That's right. Two more experienced fire fighters just gave notice that they are moving to other communities—where they will receive higher wages. We can't offer (city) adequate protection when we are constantly training newcomers. Fire fighters lay their lives on the line every time they go to work, and yet the city pays us minimum wage! That's the lowest in the entire state!

Robert: It's obvious you didn't hear the city treasurer's report! We're running a deficit operation! That means cuts in every department. (*Jabs finger at Doug*): Including yours!

Doug: Every department except for City Council! After

rejecting our requests, citing lack of money, you immediately voted a 10 percent increase in council salaries! Your income is more important than the safety of every citizen in our community! Including your own families!

Robert (*jabs finger toward* Doug): How can you expect a raise on a job where you just sit around all day doing nothing?

Doug: You have no idea what we do every day! We study reports on new fire-fighting techniques and procedures, we practice trial-run exercises for extremely dangerous situations, we check the readiness and effectiveness of all our equipment! And we're always on call—always ready to go! Fire fighters are like insurance; you recognize their importance only after a fire, but you had the protection all along. Our state legislature made this the law for the protection of the entire state—(*points finger to* Robert): including you and your family! And yet tonight, City Council has elected to reject its responsibility to enforce that law!

Theresa: Thank you Mr. Nicholson and Mr. Orwell. We must close now. (*To audience*): Now for the weather report.

Barbara holds up the remote control and presses a button. Lights go off the TV side. In the darkness, Robert, Doug and Theresa quietly exit.

Barbara You see how your father feels about fire department personnel?

Janet (*shakes head*): He'll probably never understand their importance—unless he's faced with a disaster.

Robert (*dashes in, addresses* Janet): Did you see the interview?

Janet (*nods*): Yes, I did. It was very informative.

Robert (*smiles*): That's great! I'm glad you got the message. (*Grins.*) Now you know something about the type of people who work in fire departments!

Janet: I already knew something about them, Dad. I learned it the night of the dorm fire. Their bravery, dedication and concern for lives touched me deeply.

Robert (*angrily*): You just don't understand at all!

Janet: No, Dad, the problem is, *you* don't understand. I see fire fighting as a way to put Christian love into action—a way to help people during crisis moments.

Robert: But all they want is (*rubs fingers together*) more money!

Janet: Listen to yourself! You criticize fire fighters for wanting to earn a decent wage, yet all you talk about is profits, "the bottom line!"

Robert: There's a big difference between white-collar businesses and blue-collar laborers! You have to learn to see things with the right perspective and common sense! Laborers act like they have worthwhile skills. But they don't!

Janet (*agitated*): Dad, be reasonable! Of *course* they have special skills!

Robert (*shakes head*): No, they don't! Take those shelves and that wiring; I avoided sky-high union wages by doing the work myself! No special skills were required at all!

Janet: Dad, where did you get this disrespect for laborers? Did you know that Jesus himself was a carpenter?

Robert: There you go with that Bible again.

Janet: Sure, it's loaded with good advice. Like loving and respecting everybody, including laborers, fishermen, shepherds, and tent makers. We're talking about *people*, Dad, human beings!

Robert: And I'm talking about the bottom line: profits. And profit comes from having the right job, a good public image, and influential friends.

Recorded sound *of an explosion. Each of them sway and reach out to catch their balance. It might help to have a couple of objects move, such as a hanging lamp pulled to one side by a hidden string, or a book sliding off a shelf. Each expresses shock. Barbara stares wide-eyed, hands to face, immobile, in total shock.*

Robert (*leaps from chair*): That came from the garage! (*Exits.*)

Janet (*jumps to feet, goes to Barbara, puts an arm around her shoulder*): Don't worry, Mom. We'll be okay. (*Dashes to door, returns, shouts*): There's smoke in the hallway! I'll call the fire department! (*Grabs telephone, dials.*)

Recorded voice: (City) Fire Department.

Janet: We just had an explosion in our garage, which is attached to our house! Dad had naphtha and lacquer stored inside! We're at 315 W. Fourth Street; the Nicholson residence!

Recorded voice: Did you say naphtha and lacquer?

Janet: That's right—Dad had it stored in the garage!

Recorded voice: That means we'll need the disaster squad! I'll call them on the other line and get them started! Hold until I get back with you. (*Four second silence.*) They're on the way! Where are the occupants?

Janet: Dad ran for the garage after the explosion! Mom and I are trapped in the basement with smoke pouring into the hallway. You can enter the unlocked door on the west side of the house. We're at the bottom of the stairs that are right inside the door. You'll need a fire extinguisher to get to us!

Recorded voice: I'll relay your message to the squad! Stay on the line! (*Three second silence.*)

Recorded sound *of another explosion.*

Janet: There! Did you hear that? We just had another explosion!

Recorded voice: I heard it! The squad's almost there!

Janet replaces telephone, returns to Barbara, puts an arm around her shoulder. Barbara continues to stare straight ahead, immobile.

Janet: We're going to be okay, Mom. The fire fighters should be here soon.

Recorded sound *of siren, gradually increasing in volume and then stopping abruptly just before Kevin enters below.*

Janet: They're here, Mom. (*Notices Barbara not moving, shakes her shoulders.*) Mom, are you okay? (*Bows her head*): Lord, give me the strength to hang on, and to help Mom to safety. And be with Dad. He needs your help in the worst way.

Kevin (*dashes in wearing fire-fighter's coat and hat, carrying a fire extinguisher. Sees Barbara*): You're going to be okay. We must leave quickly! (*They raise Barbara to her feet and slowly walk her toward the door.*) The other squadman is trying to reach Mr. Nicholson in the garage! (*They exit. Lights off.*)

END OF SCENE ONE

SCENE TWO: *Lights up on Robert, in a hospital gown, in a hospital bed. He has bandages on head and arms, and is propped up on several pillows. Hang sign, "ROOM 3A-49" for good audience visibility. Robert sleeps for a few moments before Barbara and Janet enter.*

Barbara (*hand up to mouth, loud stage whisper*): Since he's still sleeping, maybe we should wait in the lobby for a while.

Janet: But the nurse said it would be okay to go on in. (*They walk slowly toward Robert. He hears them and looks up.*)

Barbara (*kisses his cheek*): Oh, honey, I'm so thankful you're alive! I thought for sure you'd been killed in that second explosion! Your doctor says that after a few skin grafts,. you'll be fine.

Robert (*looks at bandages, slowly shakes head*): The last thing I remember is being thrown into the air. I thought for sure I was gonna die.

Janet: It's amazing that any of us survived. Just as the emergency van pulled away from the driveway, the garage exploded into a blazing inferno. If the disaster squad had arrived two minutes later, we would all have been killed.

Robert: How badly was the house damaged?

Barbara: Both the house and garage were totally destroyed.

Robert (*lowers head*): Oh, no!

Barbara (*goes to his side, puts her arm around his shoulder*): The important thing is—we're all alive!

Janet (*nods*): Thanks to those squad members. (*Short pause.*) Dad, Channel 9 called to let us know they have a special report on the six o'clock news about the fire. (*Checks watch*): It's time for it to start. Would you like to watch it?

Robert looks up, nods head. Janet raises remote control, pushes button. Doug, Kevin and Theresa enter and sit down at table, Theresa in the middle. Lights on TV side.

Theresa: This is Theresa Neumann of Channel 9 News with a special report on a spectacular rescue performed by our (city) fire fighters last night. Robert Nicholson, a member of the city council whom we interviewed less than a month ago regarding the controversial decision *not* to give our fire fighters a 3 percent raise, is tonight in the hospital recovering from third-degree burns. He is listed in fair condition. His wife and daughter were treated for smoke inhalation and shock and were released. With me tonight are the two fire fighters whose heroic, selfless efforts saved the lives of the Nicholson family. (*To Kevin*): How did you first learn about the fire, Kevin?

Kevin: Our dispatcher received a call from the Nicholson daughter about an explosion in their garage. Fortunately, she was cool-headed enough to tell us that naphtha and lacquer were stored inside. With that information, we knew what special equipment to grab. On our way there, the dispatcher relayed to us other facts as the daughter conveyed them.

Doug: For the first time in our careers, we knew what to expect upon arrival: Mr. Nicholson was trapped inside the garage when the explosion occurred, and the two others were caught in the basement.

Kevin: The daughter even told us which door was safe to enter. And to bring an extinguisher to reach them.

Theresa (*to Kevin*): What did you find when you arrived?

Kevin: I went directly to the west entrance with the fire extinguisher. Then I entered the basement where Mrs. Nicholson and the daughter were waiting. I found Mrs. Nicholson in a state of total shock, unable to move or talk. The daughter and I were able to get her to her feet and outside to safety.

Theresa: Are you often confronted with victims in shock?

Kevin (*nods*): Yes, it happens often in emergencies. Sometimes they are screaming hysterically, sometimes they are numb with fear. But in all my fifteen years on this job, I've never seen a victim with such faith and cool confidence as the Nicholson girl had. If she had been in shock as her mother was, I doubt that I could have gotten them out.

Theresa (*to Doug*): What was your reaction when you first heard about the explosion?

Doug: I grabbed my gear and Kevin and I jumped into the emergency van and headed for their residence. The ladder and hose truck left a few minutes later. Because of the daughter's facts, we knew what to expect. While Kevin went to rescue Mrs. Nicholson and the daughter, I headed for the garage. That's when I discovered that the explosion had shattered the door-opening mechanism.

Theresa: How did you get in?

Doug: I grabbed the axe in the van and smashed through the door. Then I stumbled along the smoke-filled aisles trying to find Mr. Nicholson. I only got a few steps before I realized a large section of the ceiling had fallen to the floor. He had to be somewhere under all that debris. I searched in the rubble several minutes before I saw his shoe sticking out. I grabbed his leg and pulled him out.

Theresa: What did you do then?

Doug: I quickly dragged him out, then checked for a pulse, but couldn't find one. In the van, I administered CPR all the way to the hospital. (*Excitedly*): Just as we arrived, I got a pulse! I still get excited just thinking about it! But if I hadn't attended that disaster squad training class, I wouldn't have known what to expect when I entered their garage.

Theresa (*surprised*): Disaster squad class? I don't understand. That was one of the things you asked City Council to approve, but they voted it down unanimously.

Doug: But that didn't stop us. The whole department chipped in and paid the way for several of us to attend a week-long class in San Francisco.

Theresa (*excitedly*): That's great! But how were you able to get the week off work?

Doug: I was scheduled for vacation that week. My wife and I had planned and made reservations for a family trip, but after talking things over, we decided to cancel our trip so that I could attend the training session. The shameful truth is we are the last industrial city in (state) to receive this training—we have to face dangerous chemical fires without the skills and equipment necessary to combat them! And, regardless of whether the city council understood or not, we felt the safety of the community was just too important to pass up the opportunity to attend these classes..

Theresa: How did those classes prepare you for the Nicholson fire?

Doug: We spent a lot of time during the week running through sample disasters. One of them was a duplicate of what we faced at the Nicholson's.

Theresa: Since Council also turned down your request for special disaster gear, did you go in without that protection?

Doug (*shakes head*): No. We decided to override their vote. Saving lives is a major priority for us, and as you can well imagine, we are keenly interested in keeping ourselves alive.

We bought one complete outfit with donated funds and decided that we would purchase other sets of protective gear as we could afford it—in spite of council's veto.

Kevin (*angrily*): To put it bluntly, we were deeply offended with Nicholson's greedy attitude and snobbish, anti-labor position! The message Council sent out was loud and clear: their salary increase was more important than public safety—and the lives of fire fighters! We decided there was no way they were going to stop us from protecting ourselves, our families and our friends!

Theresa (*to Kevin*): And that includes Doug risking his life to save Mr. Nicholson's?

Kevin: When we first arrived, smoke was pouring out from under the garage door. We could hear the raging fire inside. I pleaded with Doug not to go in; I was convinced it was certain death. (*Angrily*): And why should he risk his life to save Nicholson's? I pulled him away from the door, but he told me to go after the women. When I was gone, he smashed his way inside.

Theresa (*to Doug*): Weren't you concerned about dying?

Doug (*nods*): Of course, a fire fighter always is. But several factors give us the edge: the training we have, the protective gear, and the knowledge that comes from experience. And in my case, there is one more motivating force.

Theresa: And what might that be?

Doug: My deep faith in God.

Theresa: No kidding? How does that help?

Doug: There were two amazing facts that made me feel like God was truly watching over me. I returned from that disaster class just one week before the fire. And the disaster gear arrived the night before. It was that close. Because of that perfect timing, Mr. Nicholson is alive today.

Robert drops his head into his hands and weeps silently.

Theresa: After our interview following last month's council meeting, I'm overwhelmed by what you did.

Doug: When the dispatcher identified the owner, I remembered that council meeting and Nicholson's smug attitude and personal criticisms of all fire fighters. My first thought was, "There's no way I'm gonna risk my life for that arrogant, greedy man."

Theresa: What changed your mind?

Doug: When we got there, the strangest thing happened. I clearly remembered the theme of the sermon I heard last Sunday, "Do good unto others, even to those who don't deserve it." For a minute, it hurt to even think about it. But the memory simply wouldn't go away. (*Smiles.*) That's the trouble with sermons and Bible lessons; they force us to look at things from God's perspective—out of love. At that moment, I decided I would treat Mr. Nicholson as I would want him to treat me if the circumstances were reversed.

Theresa: So, you made your decision from a purely *Christian* point of view?

Doug: Not entirely. I took this job to serve the citizens of this community—all of them—regardless of my personal feelings. But when you get right down to it, Mr. Nicholson is one of God's children, too.

Robert groans. Barbara slips her arm around his shoulders.

Theresa: Did you ever learn the specific cause of the fire?

Doug: Yes we did. In order to store naphtha and lacquer containers, Mr Nicholson had constructed shelves throughout his garage. The shelves were too thin to properly support the heavy containers. When the top shelf collapsed, it brought down the rest of them. That ripped the poorly installed electrical wiring out of the walls, and a spark ignited the naphtha and lacquer fumes.

Kevin (*angrily*): It was the most carelessly-done job I've ever seen! And the fire could have wiped out the entire community! In fact, just as the ladder and hose truck arrived, the garage and house completely exploded. The flames were so intense, our people were unable to put them out. Both structures were totally destroyed, and the units had all they could do to protect the neighboring houses.

Theresa: Were any other houses damaged?

Kevin: The heat from the fire was so intense it melted the aluminum siding, curtains and blinds of the two closest houses. And many have suffered smoke damage. (*Bitterly*): And all because Nicholson felt he was above the law!

Theresa: Did you learn the names of the contractors who installed the shelves and wiring?

Kevin (*bitterly*): Nicholson did the work himself! In fact, he was real proud of it! He bragged to his neighbors about the $2100 in union wages he saved his company! He boasted that the job didn't require any skills at all. What an arrogant snob. (*Shakes his head.*) He'll never change.

Theresa: Storing those containers in that unapproved garage was a serious violation of the law, and posed a threat to everyone in that neighborhood. Will criminal charges be filed against him?

Kevin: I pleaded with the prosecutor to put him away! Nicholson came close to killing his own wife and daughter!

Doug: I think Mr. Nicholson has been punished enough. He has lost most of his worldly goods and he almost lost his family. One of the most effective teachers in the world is personal experience. I think Mr. Nicholson has received a Ph D in real living. We're praying for him at church. He needs all the spiritual help he can get.

Theresa: I hope he learned another lesson—to respect the skills of craftsmen and dedicated fire fighters like you.

Robert again drops his head into his hands and weeps.

Theresa (*to Doug and Kevin*): Thanks for your report. (*To audience*): Channel 9 will cover tomorrow night's emergency council meeting for developments concerning our local fire department. I expect some *real* fireworks this time! This is Theresa Neumann, wishing you all a safe and good night.

Janet holds up remote control, presses button. Lights go off the TV side. No one says anything for a few minutes. (In the darkness, Doug, Kevin, and Theresa quietly leave.)

Barbara (*to Robert*): I . . . they may have been a little hard on you, dear. (*Kisses him on cheek.*)

Janet looks away and doesn't say anything.

Robert (*shakes head, speaks slowly*): How could I have been so blind? I almost caused the death of both of you—the most loving family any person could ever have. (*Head in hands, sobs. Then*): Why have you continued to support me over all these years?

Barbara hugs him tightly.

Janet: Because we love you, Dad.

Barbara: And God loves you, too.

Robert (*voice cracks with emotion*): And Doug—he risked his life to save mine. He even brought me back to life after my heart stopped. (*Wipes eyes.*) And just last month, I publicly humiliated him. (*Shakes head*): I certainly didn't deserve what he did for me. He even used some of his own money, to attend that class. (*Hesitates, then*): And from those lessons, he learned how to save my life! (*Bows head.*)

Janet: He was just practicing the golden rule. That's straight out of the Bible. It means loving others as God loves us, including you, Dad.

Robert: As I listened to them, I thought of the dedicated workers at my own office, including the truckers, janitors, and secretaries. Each one is a vital part of the team. That's when it struck me head-on. Without them, the business would fail. And I wouldn't even have a job. (*Shakes head.*)

Barbara (*kisses him*): That's a big step in the right direction.

Robert (*looks upward*): Lord, I've been on the wrong track going the wrong way too long. It took a catastrophe to get me turned around. If I had hired a skilled carpenter and electrician to do the work, this would never have happened. But I turned down their bids.

Janet (*chuckles*): Well, Dad, I have another carpenter's bid for you. Jesus bids you to accept His gift of forgiveness and to start life over with a clean slate—what would you say to an offer like that?

Robert (*sits up, speaks excitedly*): I'd say it's too good to turn down—at any price! (*Pauses.*) Think of that; two carpenter's bids; the one who bid on the garage, and Jesus, who bids for my life! If I had accepted either one of them, that disaster wouldn't have happened! (*Quickly looks toward each in turn.*) That's the real bottom line! In fact, the *only* bottom line!

All three fall into an embrace. Lights off.

CURTAIN

One Life for Another

Characters

Sharon Ferguson; grandmother, loving, supportive, age 50-60
Dan Ferguson; grandfather, harsh, firm, age 50-60
Lisa McCoy; daughter, selfish, headstrong, age 25-35
Michele McCoy; granddaughter, happy, friendly, age 5
Beth Thatcher; friend, supportive, caring, age 40-60
Diane Nagel; long-distance friend, outgoing, age 40-60
Mail Carrier; recorded or performed live

Scenes

Scene 1: Living room with eight-month flashback in time
Scene 2: Living room five years later
Scene 3: Living room one year later
Scene 4: Living room two days later

Props

Prerecorded sound of telephone ringing
Living room with seating for three
A table with shelf or cabinet
Cradle with life-size doll
Folder with papers
Bag of cookies
Suitcase
Bible

Performance Tips

Use lights to signal scene changes and flashbacks.

For the baby, use a small doll with flexible limbs so that the one holding it can move the arms occasionally as if the baby is moving.

Telephone conversations can either be prerecorded for playback at the proper times, or callers can use a mike offstage to perform the calls live.

If you are unable to find a five-year-old to play Michele, you might use an older girl who is small for her age.

Scene One: *Sharon and Dan are seated in living room, each reading a section of the newspaper. There is a telephone and a photo album nearby.*

Dan (*looks toward Sharon*): Did you sleep any better last night?

Sharon (*nods*): I had to get up only once to feed and change Michele. That's much better than the two or three times a night it has been.

Dan (*lays newspaper down, speaks angrily*): Why doesn't Lisa get up at night and take care of her own daughter? She's only one room away from her! She's got to learn what it means to be a responsible parent!

Sharon (*nods*): You're right. But how do we get that point across to her? (*Quickly looks offstage, jumps up*): I just heard Michele whimpering. I'll go get her and be right back. (*Sharon leaves room. Dan picks up newspaper, scans for four seconds before Sharon returns with the doll.*)

Sharon (*enters room carrying baby, talking excitedly to her*): How's my sweet little granddaughter this morning? (*Hugs her tightly, walks proudly around room.*) You sure are a pretty little girl! Just like your mother when she was a couple of weeks old. And I had to get up with you only one time last night! Now that's a *real* good girl!

Dan (*fondly*): Hi, Michele! (*Goes to them, tickles baby's chin*): Yes you are a cute little girl! (*To Sharon*): You know, she *does* look just like Lisa did at that age.

Sharon (*hands baby to Dan, who sits on couch. Sharon goes to shelf.*) Let me find a picture of Lisa at that age. (*Opens album, looks through it*): Here's one! Lisa, just a few weeks old! (*Sits next to Dan, pointing.*) They look like twins!

Dan (*studies photo, looks at baby*): They certainly do! (*Pause.*) It hurts me to remember that if it hadn't been for you, Michele wouldn't even be alive today.

Sharon: I just thank God she *is* alive! (*Looks up, reflecting.*) I'll never forget the exact moment Lisa decided to give birth to her. It was just eight months ago, six months before Michele was born. I was sitting in this very room reading the newspaper when Lisa walked in.

Lights dim or go off to signal flashback. Dan leaves room with baby. Lights come back on to show Sharon reading the newspaper. Lisa enters, with a sad face, wearing a sweater or jacket.

Sharon: Hi, Lisa. Glad you could stop by this morning. Were things any better between you and Jeff last night?

Lisa: Well, maybe a little. We had a few arguments, but I guess we're going to make it. (*Sits down near Sharon.*)

Sharon: I was hoping you would have everything worked out by now. You know, it might help if you and Jeff would get back into church.

Lisa (*shakes head*): That's not for us, Mom. We've got too many other important things to do on weekends.

Sharon: We all need spiritual help, Lisa, particularly with stressful marriages.

Lisa (*angrily*): I've heard your sales pitch many times over the years. But my answer is still, "No!"

Sharon: I'm sorry if I hurt your feelings, Lisa. I'm just trying to help you.

Lisa: Let's drop it. Jeff and I have another problem to deal with now; I'm pregnant.

Sharon (*excitedly*): That's wonderful! A baby in the family! I'm so happy for you! (*Tries to hug her.*)

Lisa (*quickly pulls from Sharon's grasp*): But I'm *not* going to have a baby!

Sharon (*puzzled*): You're not?

Lisa: No, I've decided to have an abortion.

Sharon: Oh, no! Lisa! You can't!!

Lisa: Before we got married, Jeff and I agreed to hold off having kids for at least six years. We've just got too many things we want to do before starting a family.

Sharon (*very upset*): Please, Lisa, don't do this!

Lisa: It's my decision! Our marriage is shaky enough without the additional burden and stress of a baby!

Sharon: But you can't just take the baby's life! God has given you a wonderful opportunity to bring a child into the world—the same as He gave me when you were born.

Lisa: Mom, an abortion is the only answer. Since Jeff and I have both recently changed jobs, we don't even have health insurance to cover the expenses of childbirth.

Sharon: Oh honey, you don't have to worry about that; your dad and I will pay all the costs!

Lisa (*shakes head*): Thanks anyway, Mom, but this just isn't the time to have a baby.

Sharon (*pleads*): Please, Lisa. If a baby would cause problems in your marriage, I'll take care of it until things settle down.

Lisa: But you'd have to quit your job! You'd do that for me?

Sharon: I'll do whatever it takes, Lisa, to save a life—a precious life. Please, for the baby's sake!

Lisa (*hesitates*): Well. . . I don't know. . . . You're saying that you're willing to pay all the expenses, and take care of the baby if it causes a problem between Jeff and me?

Sharon (*nods head*): That's right. I'll do anything within my power to save that baby's life.

Lisa (*hesitates, then shakes head*): I don't know.

Sharon: Please, Lisa—think of the baby!

Lisa (*hesitates, head bowed slightly*): Well, if it means so much to you, I'll give it some more thought. I'll let you know.

Sharon (*hugs Lisa tightly*): I'll be waiting for your decision.

Lights off, Lisa leaves. Dan returns with baby to original position on couch. Lights come back on.

Sharon (*excitedly*): Then she called back the very next day to say she'd carry the baby full term! (*Looks at Michele*): *That* was one of the most important decisions she ever made! Dan, I'm so grateful. I'm moved to tears every time I think of Lisa almost having an abortion. This little one (*Takes Michele, hugs her tightly.*) would never have been born!

Dan: I'm proud of you, Sharon. In one sense, *you* brought Michele into this world—you helped to give her life.

Sharon (*considering*): Hummm. I never thought of it that way before, but I guess you're right. Now if we could just get Lisa and Jeff to assume their roles as parents, Michele would have a normal family.

Dan (*slightly angry*): They just don't seem to understand what it means to be parents.

Sharon (*nods, looks into* Dan's *face*): Whenever I ask Lisa to feed or change Michele, she always has an excuse. I don't mind getting up at night with Michele, but I wish Lisa would at least show her some love.

Dan (*nods head firmly*): You've just got to be firm with her.

Sharon: But it's extremely difficult to find the right words. I get all torn apart by anger on the one side, and my love for her on the other. But until she understands and accepts her obligations, we'll just have to make sure Michele is properly cared for. I'm just thankful I could quit my job to help give Michele a start in life.

Dan (*upset*): You must learn how to lay down the law! (*Glances at his watch, then points toward doorway*): Here it is—almost ten o'clock and she's still asleep!

Sharon: But we just can't order her to take the baby and go back home! We must think of Michele. She's just a helpless infant.

Dan (*nods*): I realize that. But we've got to do something! Take last night while you were at that church meeting. Lisa was watching TV when Michele began crying.

Sharon: Did she go after her?

Dan (*shakes head*): No. She just leaned over and turned up the TV so she could hear what was happening on the show. I reminded her that she was Michele's mother, and it was her responsibility to care for her.

Sharon: What did she say to that?

Dan: She angrily jumped up, snapped off the TV, and marched into the bedroom. I followed her to make sure she didn't hurt Michele.

Sharon: I just don't know how to get the message across.

Recorded sound *of telephone ringing.*

Sharon (*picks up receiver*): Hello, Sharon Ferguson speaking.

Diane (*happy voice*): Hi, Sharon. This is Diane.

Sharon (*happily*): Hi, Diane! It's good to hear from you!

Diane: And it's good to hear your voice! You can't imagine how I've missed our long talks since we moved! How is everything going for you and Dan?

Sharon: Just fine.

Diane: How does it feel to be a grandmother?

Sharon (*excitedly*): Oh Diane, it's like being a mom for the first time again! I'm learning something every day and am having so much fun, you'd think I'd never had a child of my own! How are things with your family? You mentioned in your last letter that Brian was thinking about getting married; any new developments?

Diane: Yes! He and Carol have set the date for this summer! Maybe someday I'll be a grandmother, too. Just like you!

Sharon: That's great! I'm happy for you, Diane. Believe me, it's an experience you'll never forget!

Diane: I'm glad to hear that. Well, I'd better not run up a big bill; I just wanted to hear your voice. Keep in touch.

Sharon: I will. It's really good to hear from you. Give my best to your family.

Diane: Okay. Bye! (*They both hang up.*)

Sharon: I guess I wasn't exactly truthful, but I just couldn't tell her about the problems we're having.

Dan: Well, we don't have to live with those problems, you know!

Lisa enters wearing rumpled pajamas and robe. Her hair is messed up and she appears to have just awakened.

Lisa (*yawns*): Morning. I must have overslept.

Dan (*curtly*): What time did you get home last night?

Lisa (*angrily*): Come on, Dad! I'm not a little girl anymore. Let's just drop it. Okay?

Dan: No, I'm not going to drop it!

Sharon (*pleads with Dan*): Don't be too harsh on her, Dan.

Dan: I'm not being harsh! I'm just facing facts! And I wish she'd face them, too! As Michele's mother, she's got to—

Lisa: Oh, here we go again! All you do is preach at me, just like you did back when I was in high school!

Dan: Well, it's obvious the message never got across!

Sharon (*motions for* Dan *to hush*): What he's trying to say is, Michele needs more love and attention from you. Being a parent is an every day job, Honey, but it's a job you'd enjoy if you'd let yourself; it's the most important and rewarding job in the entire world!

Lisa: Both of you treat me like I was still a teenager! Well, I'm not! I'm a grown woman trying to make a future for myself—and working desperately to save my marriage! (*Wipes eyes.*) I just don't know what to do. Or where to turn.

Sharon (*goes to* Lisa*'s side, puts an arm around her*): I'm so sorry, Lisa. You've been going through a terrible time. We've been praying for you ever since you and Jeff broke up. Why don't you come back to church with us this Sunday?

Lisa (*hatefully*): I wish you'd quit nagging me about church!

Dan (*stands, angrily*): Don't talk to your mother like that!

Sharon: Lisa, I don't know how anyone can get through life without God's help, particularly during times of crisis.

Lisa (*bitterly angry*): I've had it with both of you! *Forever*! (*Starts from room, stops, jabs finger toward* Sharon *as she speaks*): You're the cause of *all* my problems! I wish you had never talked me out of having an abortion! I'm leaving this house and I hope I never see *either* of you—or that stupid baby—again as long as I live! (*Marches from room.*)

Sharon (*weeps*): Please, Lord. (*Takes* Michele, *hugs her tightly*): Please help Lisa come to her senses! Help her to see that Michele is the most precious baby in the world, and she needs her mother and father!

Dan *hugs her tightly.*

END OF SCENE ONE

Scene Two: *Sharon and Dan are wearing different clothes but are sitting in the same living room scanning sections of the newspaper. You might wish to make some changes to the living room decor to indicate the passage of time. Michele, now five, will be entering the room soon. Sharon and Dan look though the paper silently for a few seconds after the lights come up.*

Dan (*throws down the paper angrily*): What a waste of time! It's been five years since Lisa left, and here we sit, searching the papers every day for some word about her—an accident report, a traffic ticket, whatever! (*Short pause.*) I didn't find a thing in this section!

Sharon: Nothing here either. (*Lays down paper, sighs.*) All those sleepless nights, waiting for a call. It seems like forever. And not one word.

Dan: We've filed missing person reports, we've contacted all the agencies that work with runaways, we've asked everyone we know to be on the lookout—but it's not like she's a kid who has no place to go. She and Jeff must be living and working someplace. (*Stands, throws out his arms.*) We may as well give up!

Sharon (*head in hands*): It looks like we've lost her forever.

Dan: Well, if she ever changes her mind, she knows where to find us.

Recorded sound *of telephone ringing.*

Sharon (*picks up receiver*): Hello, Ferguson residence.

Beth: Hi Sharon, this is Beth. I want to let you know what happened yesterday. I was over in (nearby town), and I saw someone who looked like Lisa. The car she was driving resembled the car Lisa had, so I followed her into a parking lot and watched her get out. Then I realized it wasn't Lisa after all, but I started thinking about her and got to wondering if you've heard anything recently?

Sharon: No, not a thing. Dan and I were just talking about the fact that we think we've done all we can.

Beth: Well, that's right. You can't force her to call. If she's ever ready to contact you, she will. I know it must be awful to think about, but after five years, you're at a point where the chances of finding her are very slim.

Sharon: Yes, that's true, Beth, unless she decides to make herself known to us. Still, we can't give up hope.

Beth: Oh! It must be so hard for you! Maybe you should just try to get on with your own lives. Oh, forgive me! That must have sounded awfully callous! (*Pause.*) I guess I just don't know what to say. One thing's for sure, we'll all keep praying for you—and for Lisa!

Sharon: We're deeply grateful for all your help, Beth. Keep in touch. (*Hangs up, smiles ruefully.*) God bless her! That Beth is a good, Christian friend! She may stick her foot in her mouth once in a while, but at least she doesn't ignore the problem like so many people do!

Dan starts to answer but Michele runs into the room carrying a bag. She is happy and excited.

Michele: Hi, Gramma! Hi, Grampa! (*Runs over, hugs each.*)

Dan: Hi, Honey! How did kindergarten go today?

Michele (*excitedly*): We played 'limpics all afternoon and I won a race!

Sharon: You did?! That's wonderful! Did you win a prize?

Michele (*holds up bag*): A bag of cookies!

Dan: How about that! Tell us about the race!

Michele: We had to race across the whole playground—and I beat *everybody*!

Dan (*excited*): That's great! I'm really proud of you!

Sharon: You have always been a fast runner. Let me show you something. (*Picks up photo album.*) I took a picture of you at a Sunday-school picnic two years ago. You won a race there, too. (*Finds the picture, points*): There you are!

Michele (*excited, points*): I'm in front of *everybody*! (*Looks at other page*): There I am on the slide! That was lots of fun!

Dan (*looks over her shoulder*): Yep! You're a regular sports star!

Sharon (*points to another photo*): And here you are at Christmastime, unwrapping "Baby," your favorite doll.

Michele: I love Baby. (*Turns pages of album backwards, stops, points to photo*): Gramma, who is that lady?

Sharon (*lowers head*): That's your mother.

Michele (*sad voice*): All my friends at school have mommies at home. But I don't have one. I wish I could have a mommy, too.

Sharon (*speaks slowly*): Honey, we've tried for five years to find your mommy, but we can't. (*Big sigh.*) Oh, how I wish we knew where she was!

Dan (*checks watch, says sadly*): I've got to go. See you later.

Michele (*looks up from photo album*): Bye, Grampa.

Dan kisses them both and leaves.

Michele (*puts down the photo album*): I sure hope my mommy will come back home someday. (*Hangs head, walks from room.*)

Recorded sound *of telephone ringing.*

Sharon: Hello, Sharon Ferguson speaking.

Diane: Hi, Sharon. Diane here. I just had to call you about some great news!

Sharon: Oh? What's happened?

Diane: Well, you know how hard Brian and Carol have been trying to have a baby. . . .

Sharon: Yes, four and a half years is a long time to wait!

Diane: Yes, and they've been to every doctor in the state. But now they've decided to adopt! They filed their application this morning.

Sharon: That's wonderful! How long will they have to wait?

Diane: Anywhere from three to seven years. It all depends on how many babies are placed for adoption and how many couples are ahead of them.

Sharon: Oh! Isn't that a shame! I just can't believe that with so many couples longing to adopt children, girls and women go ahead and abort their babies! Why can't they see that with just a few months of selflessness, they could give the baby life and make some couple very, very happy?

Diane: I don't know—it sure is a crazy mess! Well, I just thought I'd let you know their decision—please pray that a baby will turn up soon.

Sharon: I will! And thanks for letting me know their plans!

Diane: Sure thing. How's that special little granddaughter of yours doing?

Sharon: Oh, just great! She won a race in the PeeWee Olympics today—a whole bag of cookies!

Diane (*laughs*): Just what every young athlete needs! I hope I get the chance to meet her someday. She sounds like quite a charmer!

Sharon: That she is! You keep telling me that you and Jack are planning to come out here for a visit—I wish you would—we'd love to see you again.

Diane: And we'd love to see you. I'll talk to Jack about making some *serious* plans! Seems like we spend every vacation moving one of the kids or making house repairs!

Sharon (*laughs*): I know what you mean! Those great vacation trips just never seem to come off!

Diane: Right! Well listen, it's been great talking to you, but I've got to go. Write soon, okay?

Sharon: You can count on it! And keep me posted about Brian and Carol! Thanks for calling!

Diane: Couldn't wait to tell you! Bye!

Sharon: Bye! (*Hangs up.*)

Recorded sound *of doorbell. Sharon goes to side of stage and opens an imaginary door. She gasps and recoils from the door in horror as* Lisa *enters. You might change* Lisa's *hairdo and/or clothing style to indicate a passage of time.* Lisa *has a sullen, angry expression on her face.*

Sharon (*barely recovering from shock*): Lisa! What. . . where have you. . . Thank God you're alive! (*Runs to her, starts to hug her.*)

Lisa (*jerks away*): Don't touch me! I'm just here to get Michele! I've come to take her home with me.

Sharon: What . . . . what did you say?!

Lisa: I've come to take Michele home with me. Things are starting to go sour between Jeff and me again. Seeing his kid might help save our marriage.

Sharon (*shocked*): But she doesn't even know you! It's not fair for her to be caught in the middle of your fights!

Lisa: Don't start with me, Mom. She's my kid! Now where is she?

Sharon: But she was only two months old when you left—and you've been gone for *five years*! You can't just waltz in here and rip her out of the only home she's ever known!

Lisa (*loud, angry voice*): Where is she? I'm *going* to take her!

Michele enters, scared from the loud voices. She runs to Sharon, grabs her leg and looks up at Lisa, cowering with fear.

Sharon (*holds Michele tightly*): Lisa, she's *afraid* of you!

Lisa: She's coming with me! Do you understand?

Sharon: Why don't you give her some time to get acquainted with you? You could start with short visits until she gets to know you and Jeff. That would be *so* much easier on her.

Lisa: You act like you own her! I'm her mother, and I have the right to take her!

Sharon: Look at her clinging to my leg! Please think of her, Lisa. Give her a chance!

Lisa: She's *my* daughter, not *yours*!

Sharon (*close to tears*): Lisa, please! At least tell me where you live! Will she be able to go to her same school? Will you let me pick her up and take her to Sunday school? She really enjoys her teacher and her many friends!

Lisa: So, everything is still church with you, huh? I don't *ever* want to hear that stuff again! And I don't ever want to see *you* again either—*ever*!

Michele screams as Lisa tears her away from Sharon and pulls her offstage Sharon falls into a chair, or on the floor, crying hysterically.

END OF SCENE TWO

SCENE THREE: *One year later (different clothes, hair styles, subtle changes in decor). Sharon and Beth are seated in the living room. Sharon looks haggard, worn. Beth is putting papers into a folder.*

Beth: Well, that takes care of the publicity plans for VBS.

Thanks for helping with them. (*Puts folder down, reaches for Sharon's hand.*) How have you been feeling lately?

Sharon (*lowers head*): It's still rough. Losing Michele and Lisa a year ago was bad enough. Then to lose Dan six months later—(*hand to head.*) At least I know that *he* is in Heaven—not knowing where the girls are is worse than losing Dan.

Beth (*shakes head*): I can only imagine how terrible it must be. I've experienced the death of a husband, but I've never had any children walk away and never return.

Sharon (*lowers head*): Looking back, I'm surprised I've survived. I can't thank you, Pastor Olsen, and all my other Christian friends enough. You've all been so supportive.

Beth: I had a similar experience when Ted died. I'm still grateful for all the help the church gave me.

Sharon (*lowers head*): I'm still praying that somehow, someday Lisa and Michele will turn up.

Beth (*puts her hand on Sharon's arm*): Your strong faith, and your many Christian friends will carry you through.

Sharon (*nods*): I just heard from one of my best friends just last week. Do you remember Diane? She and Jack lived next door to us before they moved to (   ).

Beth: Yes, I remember them. So you still keep in touch?

Sharon: Oh yes! She's one of the dearest friends I've ever had! Anyway, she told me a year or so ago that her son and his wife were considering adopting a child. They were told they might have to wait as long as seven years, but Diane called last week to say that they were picking up their new daughter that afternoon. She was so excited!

Beth: Oh! That's wonderful! This must be a big event for them.

Sharon Yes. (*Sighs.*) Somehow, sharing in her happiness helps me to put aside my own sorrow. At least I know that somewhere in this world, families are being united and at least one little girl's life is going to be better than it was!

Beth: Sharon, I think that's a wonderful attitude for you to have. I don't know that I could be so unselfish.

Recorded sound *of the doorbell.*

Sharon (*gets up and starts toward side*): Now who could that be? I'm not expecting anyone else.

Mail Carrier: Hi, Mrs. Ferguson. You've got a Federal Express package here marked, "Photos: do not bend," so I didn't want to stuff it in your mailbox. Here you go.

Sharon (*accepts flat package*): Thank you! How very thoughtful of you! (*Closes door, returns.*) Look, it's from Diane! I'll bet she's sent pictures of her new granddaughter! (*Starts to rip packages open.*) That's just like her! She'll be the worst kind of bragging grandmother! She'll drive everyone crazy with stories—(*pulls out an 8 x 10, gasps in horror.*) No! It can't be! (*Quickly files through others.*) No! I must be dreaming!

Beth (*also shocked*): Sharon, isn't this—aren't these pictures of *Michele*?

Sharon: Yes! And this is Diane (*points*): and this is her son, Brian and his wife, Carol. And this looks too much like Michele to be anyone else!

Beth: But how can that be? Is there a letter?

Sharon grabs a letter and rips it open. She scans through the page, reading out loud in unbelieving tones.

Sharon: Dear Sharon—I'll bet you've guessed—this is our beautiful new granddaughter—not a baby after all, but a bright five-year old who had been *abandoned by her parents*! (*Stops reading long enough to look up and say*): No! No, this can't be true! (*Resumes reading*): Her name is Michele—just like your granddaughter's, and since she's accustomed to her name, Brian and Carol have decided not to change it. (*Sharon wipes eyes, shakes head, reads in a choked voice*): She seems like a well-adjusted little girl except for an occasional nightmare. She talks about her gramma and grampa all the time, but clams up when we try to question her about her parents. Of course we have no idea what she's been through, so we try not to press her. (*Looks up again, clutches hand to throat*): How could this possibly happen? Lisa has abandoned her own flesh and blood!

Beth (*equally torn up*): Oh Sharon! I—I don't know what to say! What else has she written?

Sharon (*returns to the letter in a daze*): The adoption won't be final for another three months because Michele's biological parents have the legal right to change their minds until then. But since the mother voluntarily brought the child into the social service office to give her up, we don't fear too much that she will change her mind. (*Sharon shakes her head, disbelieving, but continues reading*): Michele is a happy and loving child except when a dark cloud of memories passes over her sweet face. We don't know if she was physically abused, although she did have some rather severe bruises when we first got her. (*Sharon throws down the papers and cries out*): Oh Lisa! How *could* you?!

Beth puts her arms around Sharon, who dissolves into heart-broken sobs. The two women cry for a few moments, then Sharon breaks away in anger.

Sharon: How could Lisa *do* such a terrible thing? Give Michele away forever? Her own daughter? All she had to do was call me! Why? (*Hands over face, weeps.*)

Beth: Maybe she was so filled with guilt she couldn't face you.

Sharon (*shakes her head*): She's done it out of meanness! *Why* would she want to hurt me so much?! Why would she hurt her own daughter like that? I don't know what to do. Now I won't *ever* see Michele again. She's got a new family. And a new grandmother.

Beth: This is such a shock. . . I, I don't know what to say.

Sharon: And I can't tell Diane! She's so excited about becoming a grandmother—she would be crushed if she found out what has happened. But there's no way I can avoid writing to her—oh! What am I going to do?

Beth: Sharon, why don't you stay with me for the weekend? That'll give you a break, time to think it all over.

Sharon: I couldn't do that. It's too much trouble for you.

Beth: It would be no trouble at all, Sharon. I have that extra bedroom you can use. It's just what you need, time to think and meditate. What do you say?

Sharon (*nods*): Maybe you're right. I'll go back and pack a few clothes. (*They stand and leave as lights go down.*)

END OF SCENE THREE

Scene Four: *Lights come on as Beth and Sharon, wearing different clothes and sweaters or jackets enter the room. Sharon is carrying a small suitcase and a Bible. She places suitcase on floor, and the Bible on a table. Both remove jacket/sweater and sit down.*

Beth: Sharon, you're looking much better than when we left here Friday. These past two days must have helped.

Sharon: I'm very grateful to you for sharing your home with me! All the love you've shown me—and all those wonderful meals! How could I not feel better? I must remember to tell Pastor Olsen how much I appreciated his visit.

Beth: Were you able to make any decisions?

Sharon: Well, yes and no. It was a time of real soul-searching. (*Holds up Bible*): I found a lot of help in my Bible. . . . (*Shoulders slump*): But how can I ever forgive Lisa? I talked her out of an abortion and paid all her delivery expenses. I gave up my job to become Michele's mother for five years. And what do I get in return? Both of my girls are gone forever! It's like I'm no longer a mother! Or a grandmother!

Beth (*pats Sharon's shoulder*): I feel so sorry for you, Sharon, and there is no easy solution. (*Pause.*) I have two other friends who face a similar tragedy. Do you know Betty and Ralph Adams?

Sharon (*shakes head*): No, I haven't met them.

Beth: They haven't seen their grandson for more than nine years now. Each time their son went to pick him up, he and his ex-wife got into a violent fight. Now the courts have denied him visitation rights. Betty and Ralph have been completely cut off from all contact with their grandson.

Sharon: That's terrible! How are they taking it?

Beth: At first, they were extremely bitter. But after some soul-searching, prayer, and counseling sessions, they decided to let go of the problem and turn it over to God.

Sharon (*stunned*): How could they possibly do that?

Beth: What choice did they have? The only persons hurt by their bitterness were themselves—they had to let go of it. They found a lot of help in 1 Corinthians 13. That's where Paul spells out the many qualities of love. Two examples struck home with my friends: Love is forgiving, and love doesn't insist on its own way.

Sharon (*puzzled*): I've studied those verses, too, but I didn't see any connection to my problem.

Beth: It took them several weeks to realize that Paul's references to being selfish and unforgiving applied to them. Their bitterness toward their son and former daughter-in-law was ripping them apart. Out of love for their grandson, they let go. They're still praying for all three of them, and although they still hurt, their resentment is gone.

Sharon: Just *thinking* about trying to forgive Lisa hurts me.

Beth (*nods*): Forgiving is hard—one of the hardest things we we mortals are asked to do. Only with God's help can we forgive others. (*Sharon nods, then bows her head.*) But Sharon, just think of all the love you gave Michele during her first five years—the most important years of her life! With all the problems Lisa and Jeff were having, there was no way they could have given her that quality of love. I don't remember ever seeing a happier child in my life. Sharon, you made that happen.

Sharon (*smiles*): I never thought of it that way.

Beth: Ever since Lisa took Michele, we've been praying for a loving, supportive family for her. And now she has one. Our prayers have been answered.

Sharon (*hesitates, nods*): That's right. We *did* pray for a loving, caring family. . . it's just a different family than we anticipated.

Beth (*nods*): And you told me that Diane's family are all strong Christians—forgive me for saying this, but won't that be much better for Michele than what she probably would have had with Lisa?

Sharon (*nods*): You're right. (*Hesitates, then*): Don't worry about offending me with what you say about Lisa. For years I've chastised myself for failing with her. Her dad and I used to agonize over what we had done wrong. But you know, just before Dan died, God gave us a sense of peace about that—we did our best with her. We taught her to respect us and the Lord. But during high school she decided to go her own way. *She* chose to live the way she did and act the way she did—she never saw her dad and me treat each other the way she and Jeff treated each other. I had to learn to let go of that pain—because I was not responsible for it. I guess that's what you're trying to tell me now. Dan and I *did* give Michele a happy five years! (*Pause.*) And I'm sure I don't want to do anything now to injure the loving relationship she's building with her new family. (*Looks up.*) It'll hurt deeply, but for Michele's sake, I think I must stay out of her life. I think that would be easier for Diane, too.

Beth (*tenderly*): That's beautiful, Sharon! I've never witnessed a more powerful example of love in my life! If you're willing to voluntarily let go of your granddaughter, your love for her is very unselfish.

Sharon: Thank you, Beth. Thanks for everything you've done for me. I don't think I would have made it through this crisis without you. (*They embrace.*)

Beth: Just remember that you're never alone. Besides the Lord, you've got me; anytime you need to talk, you call me! (*Stands to go.*) I'm going to have to leave now, but I want you to promise you'll call if you need me.

Sharon (*nods*): I will, I promise.

Beth leaves, Sharon sits down.

Sharon (*bows head*): Lord, wherever Lisa is, touch her heart. Give her hope and confidence and wrap her in your love. She's hurting badly and needs all the love she can get. And Lord, help me to come to the place where I can forgive her for all the things she's done. Amen.

Recorded sound *of telephone ringing.*

Sharon: Hello, Ferguson residence.

Recorded voice of Diane: Oh, Sharon! I'm so glad you're home! This is Diane, and I've been trying to reach you all weekend.

Sharon (*awkward, hesitant*): Oh . . . . Hi, Diane. I stayed at a friend's house this weekend..

Diane: Because you were so upset, I bet! Oh Sharon, I found out right after I mailed that package of pictures! I didn't know what to do—what to think!

Sharon: You found out what?

Diane: That my new granddaughter is *your* Michele! (*Sharon* *weeps, is unable to answer.*) Sharon, you know that in most cases of adoption, neither party is allowed to know the other party's name. But Michele kept talking about her gramma and grampa and how her momma "took her away." Then one time she said "Gramma Ferguson." Of course it all fit with what you've told me about Lisa and Michele. I went and got a photograph of you and showed it to her and she was overwhelmed with joy. She shouted, "That's my gramma! Do you know where she is?" She later asked me if you could still be her gramma. Sharon, what do you think?

Sharon (*weeping uncontrollably*): What do I think about what?

Diane: Can you still be her grandma? Can you and I share this precious little girl?

Sharon: Oh, Diane, that would be wonderful! Would you be willing to do that for me? What do Brian and Carol think? Oh! I'm afraid to believe this could be true!

Diane (*laughs kindly*): Here, I think this will answer all your questions. (*Her voice is directed away from the phone*): Michele! Do you want to talk to your Gramma Ferguson?

Recorded voice of Michele: Hello, Gramma? Gramma, is that you?

Sharon: Oh, Michele! Yes, Honey, it's me! Oh, I love you so much!

Michele: Gramma, guess what?! I've got a mommy now! *And* a daddy! An' you know what else?

Sharon (*crying and laughing so hard she can hardly talk*): Tell me what else, Honey.

Michele: Gramma Nagel says I'm the luckiest little girl in the world because now I've got *three* grammas!

CURTAIN

First Things First

Characters

Mark Swartz; Preppy college student, confident, assertive
Joyce Swartz; Mother, caring, well-dressed, age 45-50
Lee Swartz; Father; quiet, well-dressed, age 45-50
Juan Ordonez; foreign visitor, mild, gentle voice, dressed in poor, but clean clothes, age 25, but looks 45 or older
Mark's thoughts and conscience; Mark's own voice may be prerecorded for playback for these two parts, or the voice of his conscience may be played by someone else, either prerecorded or performed live, off or onstage.
Seven persons at Thanksgiving service who ask questions
Extras; as many as possible, to fill out the church scene

Scenes

Scene 1: Swartz family living room
Scene 2: Church auditorium
Scene 3: Swartz family living room

Props

Living room setting with seating for at least three and a coffee table or end table with a Bible on it
Church auditorium setting, several rows of pews or seats
Wheelchair, theatrical scar (or good make-up artist)
Sleeping bag, pillow
Billfold with many dollar bills
Tape with prerecorded speeches (unless performed live)

Performance Tips

Wherever indicated, fill in the name of a local school, business, street, city, etc., to increase the impact of the play.

The settings for the living room and church auditorium may fill your stage, but when Mark makes his speeches to the audience, he should stand in a spotlight to the far right or left of the stage so that the audience can see him, but not the setting. Then when Mark moves into the scene, the lights can come up to illuminate the entire setting.

In scene two, the other characters present in the church auditorium can mime appropriate actions to what Juan is saying (also in mime) during Mark's thinking: clapping (silently) when Juan is introduced and wheeled to the microphone, shaking their heads in amazement at things Juan says, etc. Rehearse carefully so that Mark's thoughts are not overshadowed by any of the actions.

Scene One: *Swartz family living room. Joyce and Lee are seated on chairs or a couch. Juan is seated in a wheelchair and is holding a Bible. He has a gruesome scar on his cheek, a patch over one eye, and one leg is folded under to give the appearance of a missing leg. (Both legs can be covered by a blanket that leaves only one foot exposed.) Tape one arm against the actor's chest or back before putting on his shirt to give the appearance of a missing arm. Juan speaks with a foreign accent, if possible, but be sure he is understandable. These three sit quietly in the darkness as the spotlight comes up on Mark for his opening speech.*

Mark: Here it is, Thanksgiving season, 19_ _; a time when we're supposed to give thanks to God for our blessings. (*Shakes head.*) Only sometimes it's hard to find anything to be thankful for! I'm sure you've experienced the same feeling—what with life's non-stop hassles. That's how I was feeling last Thanksgiving. I was watching the (   ) game on TV at my apartment in (   ), where I attend school at (   ), when Dad called. My parents live here in (   ). Dad wanted to know if I could come home to help him with a visiting missionary. The guest speaker for the our church Thanksgiving service was Juan Ordonez, a crippled man from Uraftiland. Dad needed help getting Juan in and out of his wheelchair and in and out of the van. (*Aggravated*): That meant I had to cancel my date with Heather and drive all the way down from (   )! But, what could I do? I was stuck. So I agreed to help. Dad said he needed me home by six in order to get Mr. Ordonez to the church by seven, and I was running late so I put the pedal to the metal trying to make up some lost time. The next thing I knew, some County Mountie was on my tail, flashing his lights! (*Throws up hands.*) How can *anybody* be thankful after missing the game, breaking a date, and getting stopped by the police? But, I tried to act happy when I got home.

Spotlight goes off Mark and lights come up on the entire stage as Mark walks into the living room.

Mark: Sorry I'm late. Hope I didn't hold you up. (*Walks over to Juan, extends hand.*) You must be Juan Ordonez. I'm Mark Swartz; pleased to meet you.

Juan (*shakes hand*): Happy to meet you, too, Mark. I appreciate you for coming to help me. (*Mark shrugs.*)

Lee: We're just happy for the opportunity! It's not often we have a chance to meet a Christian from so far away!

Juan (*nods*): It's a real blessing for me to be able to come and tell you and the others about the wonderful results of your support. And I am personally deeply grateful for your gift (*indicates Joyce and Lee*), which paid my way here.

Lee: We've been working with the Uraftiland mission for many years, and now (*excitedly*), you're here to tell us personally about the work!

Joyce: In our mission studies, we've read about the urgent need in Uraftiland, and of course we hear about the internal wars on the news, but we've never actually heard a firsthand account. (*Pause.*) When I see your serious handicaps, I'm particularly grateful you could come.

Juan (*indicates missing leg*): The loss of my leg is the most difficult disability to cope with. Having only one eye (*points to it*) and one arm (*lifts it*) are much easier to handle. However, I'm very thankful I'm still alive. (*Mark frowns, puzzled.*)

Joyce (*to Mark*): And we're glad *you're* here as well! We were afraid you might have had an accident, or car trouble.

Mark (*shakes head*): No, I'm late because—(*aggravated*) I got stopped by a trooper!

Juan (*to Mark*): What is a "trooper," please?

Mark: A highway police officer. He stopped me for speeding.

Juan (*incredulous*): You mean an officer of the police stopped you and then released you without beating you up?

Mark (*nods*): That's right.

Juan: Ahhh! Then he must have threatened you with his gun.

Mark (*puzzled, shakes head*): No, he didn't.

Juan (*shakes head*): Amazing! In my country, police officers *never* release someone without first beating them, or threatening them! And often, they simply shoot them on the spot!

Mark (*outraged*): Well, that's not the way we do things in our country!

Juan (*nods*): Yes, you are most blessed in this country. (*Mark looks at Juan oddly. Lee, embarrassed, intervenes.*)

Lee: Well! (*Checks watch, stands.*) Look at the time! I guess I'd better go out and start the van! (*Exits.*)

Joyce (*to Mark*): While we were waiting for you, we learned that Juan is exactly the same age as you! (*Excitedly*): He was even born in the same month!

Mark (*looks at Juan in shock*): You're kidding! Uh, I mean, what a coincidence. It's unbelievable!

Juan: Yes, and we can both thank God that we're blessed with good health. That way we can better serve Him!

Mark (*stunned*): Good health? Ah . . . yeah, I guess so.

Juan: Yes. I thank the Lord every day for sparing my life.

Mark (*hesitates, then nods*): Ah, . . . that's . . . that's great.

Joyce (*also embarrassed, stands*): I guess we'd better get going—I think I hear Daddy with the van. . . .

END OF SCENE ONE

SCENE TWO: *Throughout this scene, Mark's thoughts are heard from a prerecorded tape. The tape player can be beside Mark (out of sight from the audience) for him to control, or it may be manipulated by someone offstage. (Could be held closer to a microphone, but would be harder to time.) Mark's facial expressions and body language reflect what he is thinking throughout. While Mark's thoughts are heard, the others onstage can either freeze in position, or continue in mime (Juan mimes speaking, audience mimes reaction in facial expressions and clapping).*

As the scene opens, Mark is standing to the extreme right or left in a spotlight with the church scene behind him in darkness.

Mark (*looks at his watch*): Well, it feels like I've been here in church for at least an hour, and I still have no reason to feel thankful; this Juan guy hasn't even started talking yet! (*Pauses.*) Those things he said at home were weird! Like being thankful for good health? And his many blessings? He looks to me like he's got one foot in the grave! (*Laughs.*) Oops! He's only got one foot! (*Pause.*) Ho hum. How much longer is this going to last? Oh! It's finally time for him to speak!

Lights come up on church scene as someone pushes Juan's wheelchair forward to a microphone. While the audience (onstage) claps, Mark takes his place in the audience.

Juan: I extend to you greetings from your brothers and sisters in the church in Uraftiland! Your prayers and financial support have saved many lives and have had a deep impact upon lives of thousands of others. This is indeed a very special Thanksgiving celebration for me as I am here before you to give thanks to our wonderful God for all He has done!

Mark's thoughts: I'm glad *he's* thankful! I can't think of any reason at all to be thankful! My grades are lousy, I have to work part time for spending money, I missed my date with Heather, and now I have to sit through this boring program! (*Stifles a yawn.*) Why didn't I just make up some excuse when Dad called and asked me to help out? (*Looks at Juan.*) He's my age? In good health? He looks more like a shriveled up old man! Why would any respectable church send *him* for a speaking tour? They need a well-dressed, good-looking speaker who could *really* touch peoples' hearts—and their pocketbooks! Ha!

Juan: Each day, I thank the Lord for His love in our lives. Your assistance has saved thousands of people, both physically and spiritually. Many in Uraftiland would not have survived without the contributions from your mission program.

Mark's thoughts (*grumpy expression on his face*): Missions!! That's all Mom and Dad ever talk about! They give money to every Christian mission program that comes along! What about me? I have needs, too! I get cut out of everything my friends do because I have to work! They belong to swim and tennis clubs, have motorbikes, and take trips to the beach during spring breaks. But I can't even own a car until I can buy it myself! (*Straightens up and assumes a pious expression.*) As a Christian, I understand the importance of helping others. But some people carry this mission thing entirely too far!

Juan: From the little bit that I have shared with you, you can see that the church is suffering from great persecution from the government in Uraftiland.

Mark's thoughts: Huh? What's he talking about? Did I miss something?

Juan: However, I am happy to report to you that God's church is not only alive, it is growing! And now, if you have any questions, I'll be happy to answer them.

Mark's thoughts: Oh no! How much longer is this going to go on? (*Person in audience raises hand.*)

Juan (*acknowledges raised hand*): Yes?

Person #1: Would you tell us something about your early life, like, where you were born and raised?

Juan: My parents had thirteen children who survived infancy, each one born in the cave where we lived, high in the mountains. The mountains of my country are a very dangerous place to live! They are inhabited by many wild animals—both the four-legged and two-legged type! (*Audience chuckles.*) In the early days, we had only cougars and jaguars to worry about, but soon the drug dealers and terrorists became a bigger threat. After one of my baby sisters was killed by a stray bullet, my father decided to move closer to town. We found a one-room shack only fifteen miles from town! It is the best home we have ever had! For the first time, we have a built-in fireplace where Mamma can cook our meals.

Mark's thoughts: A fireplace? Why didn't they just buy a microwave? That would be much faster and easier.

Juan: The house also provides us with a smooth, dirt floor, which makes sleeping much more comfortable. There is no slope, and no hard bedrock to sleep on, such as we had in the cave.

Mark's thoughts: I've got a sleeping problem, too! Mom told Juan he could sleep in *my* bed! (*Jabs finger into chest.*) That means I'm stuck with a sleeping bag on the thin, living room carpet!

Juan: The biggest problem in our home is the nearly unbearable heat. We no longer feel the fresh breeze that was high on the mountain, and when Mamma must light the cooking fire, we long for our cool cave! (*Audience chuckles.*)

Mark's thoughts: Speaking of heat (*wipes his face with handkerchief*), it's like an oven in here! Why doesn't the church spend some of that missionary money on important things—like a good air-conditioner? (*Loosens tie and collar.*) I should have stayed back in my nice, cool apartment.

Juan (*sees hand #2 raised*): Yes?

Person #2: I'd like to know what kind of health care your family has, since you live so far from town.

Juan: For most of my life, the people in my region had no hospitals or doctors. We treated our illnesses with the tonics and poultices made from wild herbs that our people have used for centuries. We had no knowledge of western medicine and practices like surgery; but even if these things had been available, we had no money to pay for them.

Mark's thoughts: He thinks he's got problems! Ever since I turned twenty-one, I've had to pay a special premium in order to remain covered under Dad's insurance policy! (*Angrily shakes head.*) And they keep on raising the deductible and reducing the coverages!

Juan: Then when I was fifteen, your mission program paid for the construction of a hospital only forty-five miles from our home. The missionaries came as doctors and nurses. As a result, many lives have been saved, and many people have accepted Jesus as their personal savior. (*Sadly*): If they could have come just eight years earlier, my four sisters and brothers who died in infancy might have survived.

Juan (*sees third raised hand*): Yes?

Person #3: Is there enough food available in your country to feed the citizens?

Juan (*sadly shakes head*): This is one of the most critical problems in our country. Tens of thousands of people die each year from starvation. Because my family lives away from town, we have land on which we try to grow vegetables both to sell and to eat. But the land is not rich enough for big harvests, and there is little rain. As soon as we were old enough to walk, we were taught to hunt for herbs, fruit, and any other edible plant—anything to stay alive. It is a day-to-day struggle. Many times when we walk to town, we see the bodies of those who have died from from starvation.

Mark's thoughts: When this is over, I'll call Heather and invite her to dinner on Sunday. (*Leans back in chair, looks upward, reflecting.*) Then I'll make reservations at (name of local, expensive restaurant). I can just taste that prime rib! (*Smiles.*)

Juan (*sees fourth raised hand*): Yes?

Person #4: Since you lived so far from other people, what did you and your brothers and sisters do in your spare time?

Juan: The little ones are allowed to play together, of course, but very early in life, we all learn to do our part to aid in the family's survival. (*Smiles*): There is very little spare time. We spend all of the daylight hours working in our garden, gathering food and wood, and carrying water. After dark, we stay inside for protection, and as long as we can see by firelight, there are tools to mend, clothes to make, and lessons to study. The little ones make games with sticks and rocks and whatever they find.

Mark's thoughts (*puzzled*): Why don't they just get a VCR for their TV? Or some computer games? Anything to keep from getting bored!

Juan (*sees fifth raised hand*): Yes?

Person #5: How is it that you speak English so well? Were you able to attend school?

Juan (*nods*): When the hospital was built, the medical missionaries started classes for those who wished to learn to read and write. My father felt that this was very important. As the eldest, I was excused from my work in the fields so that I could go and learn. Then I would come home and teach to my family everything that I had learned that day. Since the missionaries did not have books in our language, we learned to speak and read in English. Later, translators came and taught us to read and write in our own language.

Mark's thoughts: And I am learning "Engineer-speak!" When I graduate, I'll be set for $50 to $60 grand a year—easy! Of course, I'll have my low-interest student loan from the government to pay off—but I could always declare bankruptcy! Then I'd be able to keep all of my first paychecks for myself! (*Excited and happy.*) Then I can buy anything I want!

Juan (*sees sixth raised hand*): Yes?

Person#6: Do most families have cars to get around in?

Mark's thoughts: Cars! With my fifty thou a year, I can finance a new Mercedes for less than $80,000! (*Grins, gestures as if his hands are on a steering wheel.*) I can't wait!

Juan (*smiles and shakes head*): Most of the families in my country are too poor to own even a horse! Until I arrived in the United States, I had only seen two private cars in my entire life. Of course, I had seen plenty of military vehicles. The trucks driven by our police and soldiers are mounted with machine guns. (*Sadly*): We try to avoid all officers.

Mark's thoughts: Now I can relate to that! Like that trooper I ran into on the way down here. I told him that my mother had just been rushed to (name of local hospital) and she was near death! (*Grins.*) "I understand," he said, "I lost my mother last year." And he tore up the ticket and let me go! (*Chuckles.*) What a wimp!

Juan: Whenever we hear the sound of a motor vehicle, we know that trouble is on the way. Someone will be left dead in the street, or will simply disappear forever. Three years ago (*voice cracks with emotion*), both of my parents and six of their friends were gunned down by soldiers because they were singing hymns in public. (*Slowly wipes his eyes.*) Losing my parents was the saddest event of my life, but mass executions happen every day.

Mark's thoughts: How much longer is this going to last? (*Checks watch.*) I've got to call Heather and line up that dinner date for this weekend. (*Turns to Juan, listens intently.*)

Juan (*sees seventh raised hand*): Yes?

Person #7: How have you been able to survive all those tragedies? Why aren't you bitter? And, forgive me for asking, but what happened to your body?

Juan: I have survived only by the grace of God. I'm deeply grateful for His protection. (*Looks down at his missing limbs and points to his eye patch.*) These are the outward signs of the hatred that rules my country. But I cannot be bitter because inside, I have the peace of Christ—the "peace that passeth understanding."

Several years ago I was standing on a street corner inviting people to our prayer group. When I handed one man a Bible, a police officer grabbed it and accused me of breaking the law. I knew the law, but I felt God's laws were more important. When I tried to explain, he smashed his club across my face. (*Touches eye patch*): That's when I lost my eye. Then he arrested me. In prison, I was regularly beaten. The bones in one arm and leg were crushed and the torturers took delight in dragging me from room to room by my broken limbs. Infection set in and I knew that, without help, I would soon die. One night, my brothers in the Lord risked their own lives to help me escape. Of course, any escape would have been impossible without the corrupt prison officials who, for a large sum of money, would turn their heads away. My brothers carried me to the hospital, where my limbs were amputated to save my life.

Mark's thoughts: Hey, wait a minute—you were beaten and nearly killed just for passing out Bibles? That doesn't make sense!

Juan: My story is unusual only in that I survived my beatings and was allowed to escape; many in our country die at the hands of government officials. But because of Christians like you who send your sons and daughters to minister to us, and send your dollars to share the Gospel with us, many who would have died without Christ are now alive with Him.

And the power of God's living Word is not limited to changing the lives of humble peasants who must meet in secret. It thrills my heart to tell you that the officer who took my eye and threw me into prison also read the Bible he took. He was the official who allowed my escape. He later came to a secret meeting of the church. We, of course, feared that he was there to expose us and have us arrested. But he wanted to understand God's Word! He said, "Please teach me." We did, and he became a believer! How like the apostle Paul! This man who once persecuted and murdered Christians is now working quietly among the government officials to break the vicious cycle of hatred that rules our country. (*Gestures to audience*): *You*, as tools of God, are responsible for that turnabout in his life!

Mark's thoughts: That's unbelievable! (*He shakes his head in stunned silence as the lights go down.*)

END OF SCENE TWO

SCENE THREE: *The Swartz family living room later that evening. Mark is in pajamas and his sleeping bag is in place alongside the couch, but he is the far stage left or right as the spotlight comes up.*

Mark (*irritated*): As if it wasn't bad enough that this Juan guy had to spend *hours* answering everyone's questions *during* the service, we had to hang around afterwards so everyone could talk with him some more! We didn't get back home until it was too late to call Heather! And now, long after everyone else is sound asleep, I've got to try to sleep on this hard floor!

Spotlight goes off Mark and dim lights come up on the living room scene as he moves over to the rumpled sleeping bag. He gets in it, zips it up, and lies back on his pillow.

Mark (*after rolling and tossing for a while*): I'll never get to sleep out here! (*Irritated*): If Juan likes his dirt floor so much, he ought to *love* a carpeted house! Why can't *he* sleep out here instead of me?

Silence, punctuated by loud sighs as Mark rolls and turns.

Mark (*angrily*): This is impossible! (*Turns over on his side, props up on one elbow and looks out toward audience, reflecting.*) I have to admit, I can't get some of the things Juan talked about off my mind. Like forgiving that officer who almost killed him. (*Shakes his head.*) I don't understand that. How can he forgive that creep? And how can he talk about being thankful for his many blessings? What blessings? He lost a leg, an arm and an eye! (*Shakes head, bewildered.*)

Conscience: I can answer some of your questions, Mark.

Mark (*stunned, quickly sits upright*): What?! Who's that? Who's there?

Conscience: It's me, Mark; your Christian conscience.

Mark (*pulls the sleeping bag up to his chin*): Come on now—is this some kind of joke?

Conscience: No, this is no joke at all. This is serious stuff.

Mark: Wha. . . what do you want?

Conscience: I'm here to help you, Mark.

Mark: I don't need any help, thank you.

Conscience (*cheerfully*): Wrong again! You need help finding a Christian solution to your problems.

Mark: But I don't have any problems.

Conscience: You don't? You've been complaining about your so-called problems all night—all your life in fact! But those are not the problems I'm referring to. For starters, you're having trouble sleeping. You've had that problem for some time now, haven't you?

Mark (*getting angry*): What are you talking about?

Conscience: I can't count the number of times you've had trouble trying to get to sleep after committing some wrong—whether an act of omission or commission. You're tossin' and turnin' because I'm quietly nudgin' you, trying my best to get you to repent, or apologize, or whatever. But you seldom get the message. So this time, I've decided to do more than prick you—I'm going to jab the truth home—then maybe you'll let me be your guide.

Mark: Look, I'll admit I'm not a perfect Christian, but I do the best I can. Right now, all I need is a good night's sleep. So take off!

Conscience: If you listen to what I tell you and follow my directions, you'll get the best night's sleep you've ever had; I guarantee it!

Mark: Well. . . make it short!

Conscience: Throughout Juan's entire presentation, all you thought about were your own personal problems—as if you really have any! You're self-centered and on an incredible ego trip. Not once did you *really hear* what he said!

Mark (*throws up his hand*): Now that's not true! I felt really bad when he told about how he almost got killed just for passing out some Bibles!

Conscience (*sarcastically*): Oh sure! You felt so bad that you forgot all about wanting to call Heather!

Mark: OK. That's enough! I don't think sarcasm is in your job description!

Conscience: You're right, but sometimes I pick up some of *your* traits. *My* job is to help you, and the best way to help you is make sure you understand Juan's *real* message.

Mark: In other words, you're going to nag at me!

Conscience: Whatever it takes to make you understand what it means to be grateful. Do you realize that each time Juan mentioned a very critical problem, you either criticized him, or focused your mind entirely upon your own personal problem?

Mark (*angrily*): That's not true!

Conscience: Yes, it is. Here are a few examples: when he expressed gratitude for a fireplace, you ridiculed him for not getting a microwave oven. And when he mentioned the kids playing with sticks and rocks in that shack, you proposed getting a VCR and some computer games!

Mark (*pouting*): Well, it makes sense to me. That's how I keep from getting bored.

Conscience: Come on, Mark! He's from one of the poorest countries in the world! They don't even have electric *lights*, let alone TVs or VCRs! And when he talked about seeing his neighbors starve to death, you thought about getting prime rib at (name of restaurant)! I can't believe you can be so heartless—although I should be used to you by now.

Mark (*angrily*): I can't be responsible for feeding every hungry person in the world! But I care about 'em, and I pray for them—once in a while.

Conscience: That's true enough. But you *are* responsible for doing what you can do, and that's why you've been having so much trouble sleeping!

Mark: Huh?

Conscience: Look, I know you're not too familiar with your Bible, but it might help you to look up a couple of verses. There's a Bible right there on the end table; open it up and turn to James 2:14.

Mark (*picks up Bible, turns to and reads*): "What good is it, my brothers, if a man claims to have faith but has no deeds? Can such faith save him? Suppose a brother or sister is without clothes and daily food. If one of you says to him, 'Go, I wish you well; keep warm and well fed,' but does nothing about his physical needs, what good is it?" (*Puts Bible down.*) OK, I get the point; praying is not enough.

Conscience: Now turn to Luke 18:18 and read that story.

Mark (*flips through a few pages, stops and reads a few lines silently*): Yeah, I know this story. It's about the rich ruler who couldn't follow Jesus because he didn't want to give up his money.

Conscience: That's right. Read verses 24 and 25—out loud.

Mark (*looks back down to Bible*): "And when Jesus saw that, he became very sorrowful. He said, 'How hard it is for those who have riches to enter the kingdom of God! For it is easier for a camel to go through the eye of a needle than for a rich man to enter the kingdom of God.'" (*Puts down Bible and protests*): But what has that got to do with *me*? I'm not rich!

Conscience: Not rich? Not rich?!?! Look around you! Think about your life! Have you ever been hungry—really hungry? Have you ever shivered in the cold with no place to sleep? Have you ever gotten sick from drinking filthy water? Have you *ever* been without a warm bath and a clean bed? Do you honestly think you are *suffering* because you've been asked to sleep out here on this soft carpet in this warm house?

Mark hangs his head and does not answer.

Conscience: You are a member of the upper class of the richest country on earth. The population of the United States comprises only 4.7 percent of the population of the entire earth, yet consumes 25 percent of the world's resources, and generates 25 percent of the world's garbage. You alone spend enough money on *entertainment* each month to feed and clothe Juan's entire family for a year!

Mark (*interrupts*): All right! All right, I get the picture! (*Pause.*) I guess I have been pretty selfish.

Conscience: There's another fact that I must point out. Juan and you were born in the same month of the same year. By an accident of birth, you were born here, in (city), and Juan was born in a cave in Uraftiland. Neither of you had any control over where you were born. *You* could just as easily have been born into Juan's family, and he into yours.

Mark (*horrified*): I've never thought of that before! (*Pauses*): What if I *had* been born in Uraftiland? What if I had been beaten to a pulp because I gave someone a Bible? (*Hangs his head*): I've never given anyone a Bible even though there's *no* danger involved!

Conscience: Juan came here tonight to deliver a thanksgiving message from the brothers and sisters in Uraftiland to those who have helped them find abundant life—in the midst of horrific poverty and strife. You don't live in those conditions, but do you experience abundant life in Jesus?

Mark: I. . . I don't think so—I don't know! Juan does seem to have something that I'm missing.

Conscience: One thing he has is an attitude of gratitude. Are you at all familiar with the number of times God's Word instructs us to be thankful *in all circumstances*?

Mark (*grudgingly*): Seems like I have heard something about that—(*defensively*): but I don't understand it!

Conscience: In Philippians 4:10, Paul explains that part of being thankful in all circumstances is to be *content* in all circumstances. He said that he had learned to live with hunger and with being full, to live well and to suffer need. Think about those words; what does it mean—to a Christian—to learn how to live well?

Mark (*thinks for some time*): Maybe to realize that my abundant life did not come from me. . . that I could just as easily have been born into poverty and could still be thrown into it. . . that I have no right to feel proud, or superior to anyone. . . that the wealth does not really belong to me anyway and God expects me to be a good steward of all that He has left with me. . . . (*Musing*): How to live well—humm. Perhaps to be *gracious* about it—not stingy, not superior, but really glad to share with others!

Conscience: I think you're getting it! Now think about this; A few minutes ago, you admitted that you are puzzled by Juan's ability to forgive that officer who nearly killed him.

Mark: Yeah. I've heard about forgiveness all my life, but it's hard for me to forgive someone who has hurt my feelings, or ripped me off. That's a whole lot different from forgiving someone who has almost killed me—how can he do it?

Conscience: Juan has not been sheltered from corruption, from poverty, from grief. In his life, he has seen just how depraved mankind can be. Perhaps he has a better understanding of what it cost Jesus to "bear all our sins." Perhaps he understands that forgiveness is a *gift* from God—and that no man has the right to withhold it from another.

Mark (*incredulous*): Are you saying that I'm so pampered and protected that I don't fully appreciate forgiveness?

Conscience: Appreciate—that's a good word—it's similar to gratitude, or thankfulness. But to answer your question with a question, why is it so difficult for *you* to give away something that you have received as a gift, and which costs you nothing to give?

Mark (*thinking, stammering*): I. . . I don't know. I guess I've never thought of my own forgiveness as being a gift. (*Is silent, thinking for a while.*) I think I'm beginning to see why Juan is so grateful for what he has. . . he's had so little and he's lost so much. . . he's learned to value what's left. And I, on the other hand, have always had so much that I value very little of it.

Conscience: I think you're beginning to get the picture. (*Pause.*) If Juan can be thankful in spite of all the tragedy in his life, shouldn't you be thankful for at least a few of your blessings?

Mark (*nods, hand to forehead. Looks back up*): There's no doubt about it, I've been concerned only about Number One—*me*—and the *things* I have. I completely missed Juan's message of gratitude. (*Bows head.*) I feel so selfish, and so guilty.

Conscience: That's where forgiveness comes in. If God can forgive Paul and that officer who almost killed Juan, He can surely forgive you.

Mark: (*looks up, hopefully*): Now *there's* something I can be grateful for! (*Hesitates*): And I'm beginning to see that I've really been blessed. The most recent blessing is God sending Juan into my life. Then there are my parents, and the life they have given me, and the example they have set for me—if they hadn't brought Juan into their home, I would never have met him!. (*Pauses*): And there are many other blessings; Heather, good health, a job, an education, and wonderful friends. And the biggest blessing of all, the sacrifice of Jesus that allows me to be forgiven for my selfishness and thoughtlessness! (*Looks up, reflecting*): You know, I've never before taken the time to *really* think about my life; I *have* been *very* richly blessed. (*Looks upward*): Thank you, Lord.

Conscience: You're on the right path, Mark. Now for the bottom line: What are you going to do about it?

Mark (*grabs coat, pulls billfold from pocket, and removes many bills, nods head firmly*): That new car can wait! (*Holds up bills*): When Juan wakes up in the morning, I'll give this to him. And starting tomorrow, I'm going to give 10 percent of my gross income to the church—including its mission programs! (*Looks up.*) Thank you, Lord, for Juan—my brother in Christ who helped straighten out my priorities. And I promise to celebrate Thanksgiving Day *every* day! (*Smiles*): From now on, Lord, it's *first things first*!

CURTAIN

The Good Old Days

Characters

Ben Reinhart, 55 to 70 in earth years, an old-timer in Heaven

Kevin Reinhart, a younger man (30 to 45) who has recently arrived in Heaven

Props/Costumes

Ben wears old, wrinkled farm clothes, is unshaven, has tousled hair

Kevin wears modern, casual clothes, has stylish hair

Yard tools, including clippers, basket for clippings, rake, and watering can.

Enough potted flowers and plants to convey the idea of outdoor landscaping. A board or some kind of garden edging may be used to conceal the pots from the audience. (You may also choose to use artificial flowers, or simply flowers drawn on cardboard.)

A bench, or two garden chairs

Scenes: Only one; a lawn, or garden in Heaven. Ben is on his knees working with yard and garden tools. He tosses (or pretends to toss) clippings into baskets. After Kevin joins him, they talk as they water the plants, clip dead leaves, aerate the ground, etc., frequently standing, sitting, or stopping work when caught up in the conversation.

Ben (*hums or sings a hymn as he works for a few seconds, then leans back to study the plants*): Just look at that! Simply beautiful! (*Looks around*): Even after being here in Heaven for more than 160 years, I'm still amazed by the beauty of God's natural world; it truly is a Garden of Eden! (*Gets back to work.*)

Kevin enters, carrying clippers, looks around in puzzlement for a second, then heads toward Ben.

Kevin: You must be Ben Reinhart. The clerk in admissions told me I'd find you here.

Ben (*looks up, smiles, stands, extends hand*): And you must be Kevin Reinhart. (*Warm handshake.*) I received word yesterday that you'd been accepted; welcome to Heaven!

Kevin: Thanks, Ben—if I may call you that? (B*en nods graciously.*) I'm especially happy to be assigned to the Division of Flower Gardens so I can work with you; my great, great. . . I can't recall how far back you go.

Ben (*grins*): Well, let's see. . . (*begins counting on his fingers*): we're five generations apart.

Kevin: I heard a lot about you back in (your city). You may not know it, but you've become a local legend. The city has even turned your old home into a museum!

Ben (*nods*): I learned about that from your grandfather when he arrived here several years ago.

Kevin: I've heard so much about you, I feel as if I've known you for many years!

Ben: And you'll have the opportunity to meet many of your relatives in the next few days. You'll like it here in Heaven; it's filled with the most loving people you'll find anywhere.

Kevin (*looks around, smiles*): I can't get over it; no rain, no dandelions, no crabgrass—and no mosquitos! (P*ause.*) You know, working with flowers was my hobby back on earth.

Ben (*nods*): The admissions angels perfectly match people with their interests.

Kevin (*suddenly nervous, glances around*): Maybe we should get to work; we don't want anyone to see us just standing around goofing off.

Ben (*laughs and shakes his head*): No problem, Kevin! Here in Heaven, one of the most important things we can do is get to know and love each other. Here, (*gestures to bench or chairs*): let's sit down. From now on, you'll have "all the time in the world" to do the things you enjoy. (W*aves his hand around the garden*): You can spend as much time as you like in this garden—or as little.

Kevin (*grins broadly*): You mean, no work pressure or production schedules?

Ben (*nods*): That's right, Kevin.

Kevin (*excitedly*): That's great! No more hassles!

Ben (*puzzled*): I don't understand. What's "hassle?"

Kevin: Hassles are, well, like aggravations. They happen when things don't go the way you expect them to go.

Ben: I still don't understand.

Kevin: Take telephone calls for example. My boss always—

Ben (*bewildered, interrupts* Kevin): What's a tele— whatever you called it?

Kevin: A telephone? (B*en nods.*) That's difficult to explain. It's a piece of equipment people use to talk to each other.

Ben: You mean you need some kind of gadget now? When I was on earth, we just used our lips and voices. Never failed.

Kevin (*hand up, shakes head*): No, No. It's hard to describe. A telephone is used to talk to people who are not in the same room. For example, as I started to tell you, my boss who lives in (a city about 100 miles from your own) would regularly call me at all hours of the night! I never could count on a full night's sleep! It got so bad, I was forced to install a telephone answering system.

Ben (*incredulous*): You mean to tell me you actually heard his voice all the way from (*town*)? A hundred miles away?!

Kevin (*nods*): That's right.

Ben (*shakes head, amazed*): That's unbelievable! I've heard people yell from across the valley—but never one hundred miles away!

Kevin: That's what happens with a telephone.

Ben: An instrument like that sure *would* disturbed life! One of the things I liked best about living in the country, ten miles from the nearest neighbor, was the peaceful music of God's natural world. The sounds of the birds and the wind in the trees never interfered with my sleep. I can't imagine how awful it would be to hear everybody within a hundred miles all talking at the same time! I'm certainly thankful I wasn't on earth in the late twentieth century!

Kevin (*wistfully*): Yeah, I'm sure your life-style was *much* easier! (*Pause.*) Here's another example of a hassle—my shirts! They seldom fit; either the neck was too tight, or the sleeves were too short. And since fashions were always changing, I had to buy new shirts every few years and pitch the old ones!

Ben (*shakes head*): What a waste of clothes. In *my* family, each person had just two sets of clothes to worry about; one for cold weather and one for hot.

Kevin: That must have made life simple. (*Smiles.*) Now I understand why people call those "the good, old days."

Ben (*nods*): They certainly were! We didn't worry about changing fashions. (*Proudly*): My wife made all my shirts to fit, and last, and keep me warm—and they did!

Kevin: You mean she actually sewed them herself?

Ben: She sure did! We picked the flax and she wove it into linen to make our clothes.

Kevin: What is "flax?"

Ben: Flax is a plant we grew near our house. It takes three months to raise a crop, then my wife would need another month to weave the fabric, cut the pattern, and make a shirt. The shirt would last about fifteen years, and then she'd make a new one!

Kevin: Wow! I guess you never had to worry about getting your zipper stuck, did you?

Ben: Zip . . . zipper? What's that?

Kevin: It's a fastener, with metal teeth that mesh—(*waves hand*): it's too complicated to explain. But without zippers, I wouldn't have been able to keep the wind from blowing my coat open. During those awful blizzards we used to have, I could have frozen to death!

Ben (*nods sympathetically*): I know about blizzards! We'd wrap a blanket around ourselves, and during really windy snowstorms, we'd tie a rope around our waist to hold it on!

Kevin: That's certainly simple. (*Pause.*) I'll never forget the worst blizzard we ever had: on my way to work, my car got caught in a traffic jam on the freeway—seems like the worst traffic was *always* in my lane!

Ben (*looks up, puzzled*): What's a freeway? What's a car?

Kevin: A car is a travel vehicle—like your buggies, only much faster. A freeway is a wide, paved road with several lanes so that thousands of cars can travel on it at the same time—at crazy speeds.

Ben: Our lanes were never crowded. When we crossed the

mountains on foot in 1812, we met only eight people during the entire two-month journey. And each one of them was walking as slowly as we were. It really was a very pleasant trip along that old road—350 miles of beautiful wilderness.

Kevin: It *had* to have been better than our roads! Seems like they're always being repaired!

Ben: There's not too much repair involved with a dirt road. They're usually pretty smooth—except after a heavy rain, of course. Then you might find yourself in mud up to your knees! And once in awhile, we'd have to clear away a fallen tree—but we didn't have the problems you had!

Kevin: No, your way sounds much easier.

Ben: The only real problem we had was wading through those smelly swamps with six children and all our possessions. Fortunately, we weren't bothered by any snakes, panthers, or bears on that trip.

Kevin (*nods*): That was much safer. Just last month, I had an accident when I changed lanes. (*Angrily*): And even though I was badly banged up, I still got a ticket!

Ben: A ticket? To what?

Kevin: To the (city) Municipal Court! Cost me $55!

Ben (*astonished*): Just for changing lanes? That's more than a year's income! Why, we changed lanes thousands of times on that long trip and were *never* dragged into court!

Kevin: That's the way it is now, back in (city). And when I *finally* got to work that day—*more* hassles! I missed my afternoon coffee break trying to get caught up with my work, but still wasn't able to finish my assigned project before quitting time—due to some kind of work-schedule foul-up. That meant I had to finish it the following morning!

Ben (*shakes head*): I can't imagine being forced to stop a job! We always finished ours—even if it took all night.

Kevin (*aggravated*): And all for a miserable fifty thousand bucks a year! (*Waves hands in air*): That's barely enough to keep up our RV!

Ben (*bewildered*): Ar-vee? I don't understand that at all.

Kevin: RV stands for "recreational vehicle." Ours was a thirty-two-foot camper. The monthly payments alone were $320, plus maintenance, insurance, tags, and camping fees.

Ben (*amazed*): You mean you actually paid money just to camp overnight? That's unbelievable! Even on our long trip to (state) we just slept along the trail. Didn't cost us a penny! One night we even found a cave to sleep in! We always kept warm and cozy under fallen leaves.

Kevin: You certainly had it much easier than we did.

Ben (*nods*): I agree. I don't know how you tolerated all those "hassles!"

Kevin: It was tough, Ben. But, we survived. But the hassle that aggravats people the most is income taxes.

Ben: Income taxes? What's that supposed to mean?

Kevin: It means that once a year, the government reaches into the pockets of every American and grabs a tax on the amount of money he or she earned that year!

Ben: That's the craziest thing I ever heard of! Believe me, nobody *ever* tried to grab a handful of our money! Even the year of our highest income—$35—we decided where every penny of it would go; 10 percent went to needy people and the church, and the rest for ourselves!

Kevin: You really were lucky—no income taxes! Wow. Think of the paperwork you avoided! (*Pause.*) And thinking of paperwork reminds me of the endless forms we had to fill out whenever we got sick!

Ben (*shakes head*): That doesn't make any sense; what does paperwork have to do with being sick?

Kevin: We had to fill out form after form with information for the insurance company!

Ben: I'm glad we didn't have that—whatever you called it. Neither my wife nor I could read or write, and neither could most of our friends. We'd have been out of luck.

Kevin: You were very fortunate to have lived during those good old days. Later, when medical expenses skyrocketed, our insurance paid *only* 80 percent of our bills!

Ben: I do thank God for our health program—it was simple and practical. We picked herbs and made our own tonics. *Never* had any paperwork!

Kevin: I'll bet *that* made life easy! Getting medicine was another problem for us. We had to drive clear over to (mall across city) to find a drugstore that accepted our drug card!

Ben (*puzzled*): I don't understand. What's a "mall?" What's a "drug store?" What's a "drug card?"

Kevin: A mall is a building, or group of buildings that contain many stores, each one selling a certain kind of product.

Ben (*puzzled*): Give me an example.

Kevin: Well, one store sells clothes, another sells books and magazines, and a "drugstore" sells drugs and medicines. We wasted a lot of time just walking between each store and looking at all the stuff. And I *always* got stuck in a long line when I went to pay my bill!

Ben (*shakes head*): It's hard to believe how bad things have become. We had just one general store that handled everything. We didn't waste any time going from store to store, and it was *very* convenient; just two hours by horseback.

Kevin: Two hours?! Well, I guess you had to pay *some* price for all that quiet solitude. Still, I sure wish we had it that simple. (*Pause.*) The biggest medical expense of all occurred when the twins were born; that hospital bill was out-of-sight!

Ben (*puzzled*): You had to pay for your children? I've heard of buying calves, but never children! Ours didn't cost us a penny! But why were you in a hospital?

Kevin: I took my wife there to deliver our babies, of course!

Ben: You mean she didn't have them at home?

Kevin: No, of course not, Ben. Who would help deliver them?

Ben: Well, our neighbors always helped delivered our children—all fifteen of them!

Kevin: Oh, you mean you used a midwife. Well, how much did that cost?

Ben: Nothing—well that is, she never *charged* anything! Of course, we always tried to show our gratitude with some small gift, and my wife would do the same for them.

Kevin: I wish we could have had that kind of arrangement. We could have saved a pile of money—not to mention that frantic, twenty-mile trip to the hospital!

Ben: Twenty miles! It's a good thing we didn't have to go that far to have our babies; in a four-hour trip by horseback or buggy, we'd have lost all of them!

Kevin: Yes, it was much easier—and cheaper—having them at home. But what did you do if something went wrong?

Ben: We prayed. And I'll be the first to admit that God was very gracious to us. I didn't lose my wife in childbirth like some husbands did, and only three of our children died at birth. Ten of the other twelve lived long enough to reach adulthood! We thanked the good Lord many times for our blessings.

Kevin (*smiles*): How I wish I'd been born earlier. Besides the cost of the twins' birth, my wife and I had to conform to those crazy rules set by the nursing supervisor.

Ben: You mean someone was hired just to supervise nursing for your wife? (*Shakes head, bewildered.*) Nursing just came naturally to our mothers—no supervision required at all.

Kevin: No, the nursing supervisor was a part of the staff at the hospital, part of the reason why having a baby cost so much. And as if expenses weren't high enough after the birth of the twins, when we got home from the hospital, we found that our microwave *and* furnace had quit at the same time! It cost us an arm and a leg to get them repaired!

Ben: What does "micro. . . " whatever mean? And why did you have a *furnace* in your home!?

Kevin: Well, we cooked our meals in the microwave oven, and heated the house with the furnace. And since they were both broken, we had no way to eat and no heat.

Ben: That's the way people live down there now? That's absurd! The 1800's were *much* simpler. Our fireplace was *always* dependable. It never failed as long as I cut enough wood. I started the fire before sunrise. The house was warm and breakfast ready to eat in less than two hours—at no cost at all! And at night, to keep us warm in bed, we just heated up some large rocks in the fireplace, wrapped them in a towel, and put them in our beds—kept us warm all night.

Kevin: That sure sounds simple. But until we got our microwave repaired, we had to eat out—more expenses!

Ben: What?! You paid money to eat outside?!

Kevin: Of course! Do you think you can eat out for free?

Ben: We certainly did! We ate out all the time—nuts, roots, fruit from the trees—no cost at all.

Kevin: Oh! Well, I'm not talking about *picnics*! I'm talking about restaurants and fast-food places—although we always had to wait in line even at the fast-food places!

Ben: How can one place grow food faster than another?

Kevin: Oh, they didn't *grow* it, they just prepared it. You're supposed to be able to pick up prepared food without waiting at a fast food place, but sometimes we had to wait in line as long as ten minutes to get our order.

Ben: That is terrible! When we ate out, we *never* had to wait in line. We just picked the fruits and nuts, and ate them!

Kevin (*grins*): Well, that's what I call fast food! But we don't pick many fruits and nuts down in (   ) anymore. But, getting back to my story, the appliance breakdowns were just the beginning of our problems! Later, I was in the TV room watching the most important baseball game of the year—in the world series—when the electric power went off!

Ben (*has been lost since* "TV"): Wait a minute! Hold your horses! What *are* you talking about? What is a tee vee room? What is bezbal, and what is lectri—whatever you said?

Kevin: A TV room is where we have our TV set—don't ask me to explain what a TV is! Baseball is a game involving two teams of at least nine players. And *electricity* is. . . well, let's just say that it's an invisible source of power that makes it possible to bring the baseball game into our room!

Ben (*totally lost, trying to comprehend*): Wow! A room large enough to hold both teams!

Kevin: Well, actually it's. . . Oh, forget it—it's too complicated to explain. The point is, we can't do *anything* without electricity and with the power off, everything went, including our lights and air-conditioning!

Ben: Didn't you have other candles available?

Kevin: No, we didn't have *any* candles.

Ben: That's too bad. We always made enough to last us a couple of months. But what's air-conditioning?

Kevin: That's a unit—a machine—that keeps our house cool on hot, sticky days.

Ben: I don't understand.

Kevin: It's kind of hard to explain—

Ben: Seems like a lot of your fancy machines are hard to explain. When we got hot, we just opened all our doors and windows—the breeze cooled us off in no time at all.

Kevin: That's really neat, but there aren't many cool breezes in (   ) these days. And, as if being without our electricity wasn't bad enough, two days later, the city cut off our water supply so they could repair the lines! That meant no drinking water and no showers!

Ben: How in the world could anybody cut off the supply of water? That comes from underground springs that run into wells. Twice a day, I simply lowered a bucket into our well and got all the water we needed—winter and summer! Life has *really* gone downhill!

Kevin: All I know is, the city cut off our water, and without water we couldn't even take a bath.

Ben (*bewildered*): Why not? We took our baths—once a month or so—in the creek. Except in winter, of course, when it was covered with ice. Nobody *ever* messed with our water supply!

Kevin (*shakes his head sadly*): Times have really changed since the good old days. But what was worse, without running water, we couldn't use our commodes!

Ben (*puzzled*): How can a washstand quit working?

Kevin: I said, "commode," not "washstand."

Ben: But a commode *is* where people wash themselves!

Kevin (*shocked*): You used your *commode* to take a bath?

Ben (*nods*): Every morning. For a real bath, we used the creek.

Kevin (*amazed, shakes head*): I never heard of such a thing. We always use the commode as a toilet.

Ben: Right there in the house? We had more sense than that! We used outhouses—located *far* away from our houses. I built ours seventy yards downwind.

Kevin: You went *outside* to use the toilet? *Seventy* yards from the house? Even in the winter?

Ben (*nods*): That's right, and I'm sure glad I died before people started using the toilet in their houses! (*Grimaces.*)

Kevin: Ben, how old were you when you died?

Ben: I'd just turned thirty-nine.

Kevin: I would have guessed you to be ninety-five from your gnarled hands.

Ben (*not offended, examines his hands*): Oh no! That's just from good old hard work! Most of my friends died when they were much younger. Illness, starvation, shoot-outs, tangles with the wildlife, and accidents all took their toll. At the time, I thought ours was the toughest life possible, but I see now that I was wrong. I don't know how you tolerated all those aggravations.

Kevin: It was tough, Ben. I've always envied your hassle-free life. I recall my last visit to the museum, your former home; soft, electric candlelight, gas-fired fireplace logs, and costumed hostesses waiting to show the guests around the house. That was *real* comfortable living!

Ben (*chuckles*): Right! As long as you remember that we used *real* candles and *real* logs! (*Pauses.*) But I think we did have life easier than you did. We were forced to rely on God to supply our every need. I'm convinced that when survival was a struggle, it was much easier to grab the Lord's promises and hang on for dear life. And that's all it took. To us, Thanksgiving Day was every day as we gave thanks to God for His blessings in our lives. And as short as our money was, we always had enough to set aside 10 percent to share with those who were less fortunate.

Kevin (*thoughtfully*): You know Ben, you have something there. Our modern conveniences may have cluttered up our lives—and pushed God out. We weren't nearly as aware of His presence and His continual blessings as you were. (*Works silently for a while.*) I think I'm learning to better appreciate the fact that I'm here by God's grace, and not because of anything I've done to deserve this reward!

Ben (*chuckles*): Son, I'd say that's a pretty big insight for your first day in Heaven—keep up the good work!

CURTAIN

The Road to Bethlehem

Characters

Art Kenton; businessman, bossy, greedy, and snobbish, well-dressed, age 45-60

Shirley Kenton; wife, sensitive and caring homemaker, well-dressed, age 45-60

Joe Christian; carpenter, sensitive and caring, poorly-dressed, age 20-30

Mary Ann Christian; wife, mother, sensitive and caring, poorly-dressed, age 20-30

Five Voices; recorded for playback, or live offstage

Props

Telephone and TV
Two chairs or sofa
Doll, blankets and pillows
Heavy winter clothing, crutches
TV *Guide*, newspaper, remote control
Facsimile of front seat of car, including steering wheel
Cassette with taped voices for telephone conversations, TV program, radio announcer, and sound of car crash (check the public library for recorded sound effects)

Scenes

Scene 1: Family room of wealthy couple on Christmas Eve
Scene 2: Front seat of car
Scene 3: Deserted farm stable
Scene 4: Family room same evening

Performance Tips

Your stage will be split into three settings; a family room on one side, a deserted barn on the other, and the driver's seat of a car, centerstage. (You may choose to carry the car seat onstage between scenes, so that it will not interfere with the other action.)

The family room is that of a wealthy family and contains at least two chairs or a sofa, a telephone (near Art's chair) and TV (with screen hidden from audience view). On a lamp stand or coffee table will be a newspaper and a TV *Guide*. Some Christmas decorations would be appropriate.

For the car setting, you might find a car seat and steering wheel at a junk yard, or wrap a blanket around a chair to resemble a car seat. A chair with some spring to it will allow your driver to bounce around. If you don't use a real steering wheel, make a facsimile from wood or cardboard and either attach it to some kind of support, or have your actor simply hold it in his hands. The best arrangement would be to attach it to the driver's seat so that when the car "turns over," the actor will not have to keep holding the wheel in place.

The deserted barn setting needs just a few rough boards in the background and some old blankets and pillows on the floor.

Use lights to signal scene changes or end of scenes.

SCENE ONE: *The lights come up on* Shirley *and* Art, *seated in their family room.* Shirley *scans the newspaper while* Art *stares into space—bored and restless.*

Art (*fidgets silently for a while after scene opens. He has a grumpy expression on his face, and during his figeting he crosses his arms in front of his chest. Finally he speaks*): Here is it Christmas Eve! The most boring time of the year! A *total* waste of time!

Shirley (*continues looking at paper while speaking*): I'm sorry you feel that way, Dear. To me, Christmas is the best time of the year! This is when we celebrate that special night in Bethlehem when Christ was born.

Art (*shakes head*): I don't feel like celebrating *anything*.

Shirley (*looks at* Art): You need to take some time off work—get your mind off business, relax!

Art (*impatiently*): How can I take time off? With two businesses to manage, there's no time for *anything* but work!

Shirley: That's *exactly* why you need to take some time off—to consider your many blessings! You don't appreciate what you have—and you haven't been to church now in (*looks up, reflecting*) let's see . . . it's been more than eight years.

Art (*angrily*): But I *do* take time off—*every year*! Every Christmas Eve, I leave work two hours early just to be with you. And when the kids get in on Christmas Day, I spend three hours with them! That's five hours every year!

Shirley (*semi-sarcastically*): We appreciate that, Dear. We know it's a real sacrifice for you. (*Sighs.*) I look forward to these two days every year, just to be with you. (*Pause.*) This year, the kids will be staying over another day. Could you arrange to be here with them until they leave?

Art (*shakes head*): Sorry, no can do. I always use the day after Christmas to be by myself at the office. It's the *only* uninterrupted time I have to plan the next years' budget for the store and the apartment complex!

Shirley (*sighs, returns to newspaper. After a moment*): Here's an article that's right on target. (*Reads aloud*): "As we prepare for Christmas, the celebration of Jesus' birth, we should consider those shepherds and Wise-men who sought Him in Bethlehem. The shepherds put aside their worldly responsibilites and followed the road to Bethlehem to find and worship the babe in the manger. The Wise-men invested great amounts of time and money to pay homage to the child who would be King. That's the message for us each and every day; follow the road to Bethlehem seek out and worship Immanuel, 'God, who is with us'." (*Looks at Art excitedly*): There's your answer, Art—follow the road to Bethlehem! You could start by coming back to church. An excellent Bible-study group for men has recently been organized—

Art (*interrupts*): Can't you understand? I'm responsible for two business operations! There's just no time left for church!

Shirley: Well, how about selling the Kenton Apartments? That would give you more time.

Art (*shakes head violently*): Are you crazy? I'd lose (*stops, calculates on fingers*) I'd lose about $40,000 a year!! We'd have only $50,000 a year to live on! That's barely enough to keep food on the table!

Shirley: Oh Art! We're a long way from starving to death! But that reminds me of all the helpless and homeless people right here in our own community who *are* starving—and we're doing absolutely nothing to help them.

Art: We don't owe them a thing! You don't know the *real* world like I do. Out there, it's everybody for himself—grab all you can get, anyway you can. That's what it's all about!

Shirley (*hand to lowered head*): I can't believe you can be so heartless—and greedy. Particularly at Christmas.

Art: Call it what you want. I'm just being practical. (*Glances at watch*): It's getting late. I'd better see if Fran is home yet—I want to know what sales were like after I left.

Art dials the number, listens, gestures excitedly during the conversation. Shirley reads paper, occasionally shakes and lowers her head, wipes her eyes during Art's later conversation.

Recorded voice of Fran: Hello, Fran Henderson speaking.

Art: Hi, Fran. I hope I didn't interrupt anything.

Fran: Oh, hello, Mr. Kenton. No, we just finished wrapping our gifts for tomorrow and were climbing into bed.

Art: Sorry to bother you at home, but you know how it is—the business comes first! Since I left early today to be with Shirley, I was worried about how sales went tonight.

Fran: We had the best Christmas Eve we've ever had! Customers were spending like crazy! The cash register receipts totalled over $17,000!

Art (*shouts*): That's great!

Fran: As you've often said, "A green Christmas beats a white one every time!"

Art: You've got that right! The green stuff is what Christmas is all about!! With that sales record, I might even increase my charitable contributions—up to $25 a year. (*Chuckles.*) I must keep up my public image, you know! See you Monday, Fran—and thanks for the great news! (*Hangs up, beaming.*)

Shirley (*looks at Art*): What can I do to help you understand what Christmas is *really* all about?

Art (*rudely*): Let's worry about that later! Right now I've got some urgent business to take care of! I told Janet to get a couple of deadbeat tenants out of one of my apartments—by whatever means were necessary. I need to know if she followed my orders.

Shirley: Are those "deadbeats" the couple you told me about? The ones who are about to have a baby?

Art (*nods*): They're the ones. They're more than four months behind in rent.

Shirley (*upset*): How can you stand to evict people—especially a woman who's pregnant?

Art: This is business, Shirley. The way I see it, they're *tenants*, not people.

Shirley: Couldn't you at least have waited until after Christmas?

Art (*shakes head*): Look, there's nothing in their lease about Christmas, or being pregnant. But the lease is very clear about getting evicted if they don't pay their rent. Four months is a *long* time—too long! (*Dials telephone, listens.*)

Recorded voice of Jan (*very sleepy*): Hello, Jan speaking.

Art: Jan! This is Art. Are you okay? You sound like you're not feeling well.

Jan: I'm fine, Mr. Kenton. It's just that we've been asleep for over an hour now.

Art: Oh—sorry. But if this wasn't important, I wouldn't have called. First, I want to tell you about our sales today down at the store. We had our best Christmas Eve on record! We took in over $17,000!

Jan: That's great! That full-page ad supporting the Good Samaritan Agency really paid off. I heard many compliments about it from our tenants here at Kenton Apartments.

Art: And that spot on the Christian radio station didn't hurt either. (*Laughs.*) We're helping them spread that Christmas spirit—right into our cash registers! By the way, you did a great job decorating the apartments.

Jan: Thanks. It makes the tenants happier. And that translates into reduced turnover and bigger bucks.

Art: Good thinking! Maybe they'll quit complaining about those stopped-up toilets and lack of hot water.

Jan: We haven't had a complaint for over a week now.

Art: That's great! Listen, the other thing I called you about is that couple in apartment 58; I've forgotten their names.

Jan: Joe and Mary Ann Christian.

Art: Right. Have you kicked them out yet?

Jan: I forced them out around noon today.

Art: Great! Were they still complaining about their furnace not working?

Jan: That's all Mary Ann talked about. I told her we weren't running a public welfare agency and that we'd fix their furnace when they paid their four months back rent—and not until then!

Art: That's the way to handle it.

Jan: That's when she started sobbing, and mumbling something about Joe breaking his leg on his carpenter job. That was their excuse for not paying the rent. I told her that was entirely their problem.

Art: How did she react to that?

Jan: Oh, she cried even harder! Told me how they were freezing to death without any heat. That's when I told her what you said, that it was going to be even colder out there on the streets—so it's pay up, or get out!

Art: Good job! That's the only way to handle deadbeats.

Jan: Joe got all choked up. He pointed to Mary Ann and pleaded, "But our baby's due any day now." I gave him ten minutes to shove off. They grabbed a few things and drove off toward the Good Samaritan Agency, leaving everything behind. It was mostly trash. So I pitched it into the dumpster out back.

Art: Well, there's nothing else we can do with the junk people leave behind—after all, I'm not running a storage center—or a charity house! Now that they're gone, go ahead and replace that furnace. It's too dangerous anyway. If it blew up, the fire could destroy the entire complex—that would be 105 apartments up in smoke. That would be an awful mess to clean up! Besides, if we do it now, I can take a tax deduction this year.

Jan: I'll take care of it immediately.

Art: Have you mailed out the notices on that 30 percent rent increase yet?

Jan: They're all set for Monday's mail. I wanted to wait a couple of days. That Christmas spirit from all those decorations and carol music in the hallways might soften them up for that 30 percent shock.

Art: Good planning! OK, that's it for now. You can go on back to bed. (*Hangs up.*)

Shirley sits with her head bowed, occasionally wipes her eyes.

Art (*fails to notice her*): Let's see. . . 30 percent increase on 105 units means about. . . $15,000 more profit next year. (*Turns to Shirley*): How about that! $15,000 more income next year!

Shirley (*looks up, crying*): How can you do that, Art?

Art (*doesn't hear her*): Now, how can I use that $15,000?

Shirley: Art, please listen to me. I can't take anymore of this. I feel incredibly guilty about the new car you bought me for Christmas.

Art (*stunned*): Guilty? I don't understand. You *needed* a new car! Your old one was two years old and had more than 25,000 miles on it! And besides, the new car cost only $38,000! That rent increase alone will pay for almost half of it!

Shirley: But that Christian couple—humm, interesting name—I wonder if they really are?

Art: What are you mumbling about?

Shirley: I was saying that the couple you evicted *really* needs help! They're *desperate*, Art! I'd rather sell my new car and give them the money.

Art: Look, you got what you deserve—a new car. And they got *exactly* what they deserve—evicted for overdue rent!

Shirley (*hand to forehead*): When you gave me that gift certificate for $5,000, I was really happy. I thought I needed a lot of things, including a new fur jacket, but I've lost my desire for new things after hearing about them. I've decided to give them the money instead.

Art: Don't be ridiculous, Shirley! (*Looks upward, shakes head.*) Here it is, Christmas Eve. We should be talking about happy things! (*Pause.*) Are you all set for Becky and Eric tomorrow?

Shirley (*nods*): We're all set. I got Becky a refrigerator, a new microwave, a $2,OOO gift certificate, and a crib for our new grandson. And for Eric; a washer-dryer, stove, and $2,000 in cash.

Art: That's great! We're all set for the big day!

Shirley (*checks watch, picks up* TV Guide, *scans briefly*): Here's a TV special that might get us into the Christmas spirit—but it's almost over. (*Uses a remote to turn on* TV.)

Recorded voice from TV: Our last visit tonight is with the director of the Good Samaritan Agency. Tonight, there are forty families here, enjoying their first full meal in weeks, thanks in part to a large Christmas donation from the (   ) church here in (   ). (*Pause in tape while* Art *speaks.*)

Art: Why do they have to ruin a beautiful holiday by showing that depressing stuff? (*Points to* TV): Those must be the laziest people in town. If the state would just drop all those welfare programs, they'd be forced to work for a change! It reminds me of that lazy couple I just evicted!

TV: As Director Brooks said earlier, "This is the season for sharing God's blessings, particularly with families in desperate need." Many of these people are homeless, especially those without jobs. Like this couple over here. She's pregnant and expecting the baby at any time—it could come tonight. He was working for the Landmark Construction Agency when he fell off the roof and fractured his leg. Out of work for three months now, they've been unable to keep up with rent payments, and just tonight—on Christmas Eve—they were evicted from the the Kenton Apartments.

Shirley (*shocked*): Oh Art! They must be that Christian couple! (*Bows her head into her hands, weeps.*)

Art (*defensive, uncomfortable*): Shirley, you're making too much out of this. It's not like they're out on the streets. They've got a place to stay.

Shirley continues weeping, hands over face.

Art (*aggravated*): I can't believe this! (*Goes to* TV, *snaps off, paces around the room.*) What other Christmas programs are on—anything worth watching? Are there any Santa Claus stories? We need some happiness—some *real* Christmas spirit.

Shirley (*wipes eyes, slowly opens* TV *Guide, studies closely*): They're all about the same subject—helping the needy. (*A little angry*): And *that is* the *real* Christmas message!

Art: Oh, phooey! Thinking about poor people takes all the joy out of the holiday season!

Shirley (*shakes head, angrily*): Only if you're an incredibly selfish person! (*Stands up.*) I can't take anymore of this! Art, you have no idea what Christmas *really* means! I'm going to bed! (*Leaves.*)

Art (*sheepishly looks at* TV Guide): Here's a good one, "Christmas Trees Around the World." (*Looks at watch.*) Starts in thirty minutes. (*Looks around deserted room, sighs.*) Some Christmas Eve! (*Pause.*) Guess I'll take a nap. Maybe I can dream up a way to make more money next year. (*He stretches out on the sofa, or slumps into the chair, gets comfortable, nods off, goes limp, starts snoring. Lights could be dimmed slowly as he is falling asleep.*)

END OF SCENE ONE

SCENE TWO: *When the lights are off, Art puts on an overcoat, scarf and hat, then walks to car seat which is on, or which has just been carried to, the front of stage. He sits at a slight angle, facing the audience and puts his hands on the steering wheel. When the lights come up, Art acts as if he is driving, moving hands and head accordingly. One foot is raised slightly as if on the accelerator, and changes quickly to press down on brake when indicated. One not-too-bright spotlight on Art will add to the fantasy and scariness of this scene.*

Art (*leans forward, squints, as if unable to see road clearly*): This snow is *really* coming down! If I'd done my shopping for Shirley yesterday, I wouldn't be out here in this mess on Christmas Eve trying to find the shopping center. (*Leans forward, staring intently.*) It's getting worse and the road is slick! Whoops!! (*Touches brake pedal, moves around as if in a skid.*) Almost slid off the road! This is terrible! (*Pause.*) I'd better see if I can get a weather report. (*Reaches over and pretends to turn on radio.*)

Recorded radio voice: To repeat, we are now under a snow emergency. All roads in (   ) and (   ) counties are *closed*! Emergency road crews are working, but in the past hour we've received dozens of reports of stranded motorists. Don't leave your house! If you have an emergency, the police, fire, and hospital units will respond with four-wheel drive vehicles!

Art (*angrily snaps off radio*): I'll get there one way or the other! (*After a few more slippery turns, he yells*): I can't even tell where I am! I'm lost! (*Pause, fearful driving*): I can't even find a place to stop on this icy road! (*Leans forward, squints eyes.*) There's a sign—maybe it'll tell me where I am. (*Stares, squints, reads*): Bethlehem—three miles. Bethlehem!? Never heard of it. (*Shakes head.*) What am I going to do? There's no way I'll find that shopping center in this blizzard. Wait a minute! There's a light—what?! (*He screams. His body jerks around as if car is swerving. He yells*): I've lost control! I'm sliding off the road! That tree! I'm going to hit it!

Recorded Sound of a car crash.

Art (*rolls over on side, holds chair above his body—or chair rolls over on side as* Art *does.*) AAAAIIIII! I've rolled over! I'm in a ditch! (*Struggles to get free.*) I can't get out! (*Tries to open door.*) I can't even open the door! I'm pinned in here! (*Moans, looks around*): I'll freeze to death out here! (*He struggles some more, without success.*) Oh, Lord, I'm gonna die! I need Your help—desperately! Please don't let me die! Help me out of this mess and I'll be the best Christian You've ever seen! I promise!! (*Stares ahead, puzzled.*) What *is* that light? I saw it just before I crashed. It—it looks like a star—only bigger, over there, in the East.

Joe (*wearing tattered coat and cap walks slowly on crutches, leg held stiffly. Stops, bends over, looks at* Art): Hey! You in there—are you okay?

Art (*startled, nods very slowly*): Oh! Thank God you've come! I think I'm OK, but I can't get out the car. Who are you?

Joe (*starts tugging on door handle*): My name is Joe. (*Grunt, huff.*) Sure am glad someone put that lighted star on the barn over there. Otherwise, I would never have seen your car in this terrible storm.

Art: A star! That must be what I've been seeing!

Joe (*still tugging*): The glass is all broken out, but I can't get this door open. Are you hurting anywhere?

Art: I'm too numb to feel a thing. (*Pleads*): Please help me!

Joe (*straightens up and looks around*): OK. I think I saw a donkey in that field over there (*points*). I'll try to get it. Then, with a rope over that tree limb and the donkey pulling, maybe I can get your door open and drag you out.

Art (*pleading*): Oh, please try! Please get me out of here!

Joe: Sure thing, mister. You just try to stay warm. I'll be back just as quick as I can! (*Joe walks away as fast as he can with his bad leg as lights go down and off.*)

END OF SCENE TWO

SCENE THREE: *In a deserted barn,* Mary Ann *is seated on a couple of blankets on the floor, holding a doll wrapped in thin blankets.* Joe *is stretched out beside her.* His *crutches rest on the floor nearby. Scene opens with* Art *standing near them, hat in hand.* Lights *come up*.

Art (*humbly*): I can't thank you enough for saving my life.

Joe: I'm just thankful that everything came together the way it did: our baby woke us up, that lighted Christmas star showed me the way to your car, and that donkey was able to pull your door open. Otherwise, you probably would have frozen to death in your car.

Art: But why were *you* outside in this terrible storm?

Mary Ann: You can thank him (*points to baby*) for that. Joe and I were had just dozed off when your car hit the tree, but the sound of the impact frightened the baby so badly that he screamed, and got to crying so hard that Joe decided to get up and go look. As soon as he left, the baby stopped crying.

Art: That's unbelievable! I'm alive because of your baby! (S*quats down to look at baby.*) How old is he?

Mary Ann: Just two hours old! He was born at midnight.

Art (*sits down in shock*): You mean he was born right here?

Mary Ann (*nods and says proudly*): Joe delivered him.

Art: But why didn't you go to the hospital? Or call a doctor? And why are you *here*, in this old barn in the first place?

Mary Ann: Joe lost his job when he broke his leg, so we have no health insurance. And we were kicked out of our apartment earlier today. We got some dinner at the Good Samaritan Agency and were on our way to Joe's sister's place in (   ) when our car broke down. The storm had already started and I was already in labor—so, we had no choice but to crawl in here and do the best we could.

Joe: At first we were scared. Then we decided to just trust God. To tell you the truth, we though it was kinda neat that our baby was going to be born in a barn, on Christmas Eve!

Mary Ann (*excitedly*): And, our car broke down on Bethlehem Road! All of these unusual coincidences made us feel like God was really with us all along!

Art: But it could have been disastrous. (L*ooks around, thinking*.) Why were you kicked out of your apartment?

Joe: We couldn't pay the rent. I can't get work until my leg heals and Mary Ann's had a hard time with the last few months of this pregnancy. We don't really blame the manager—she had to do what she had to do.

Mary Ann (*a little angry*): Actually, in some ways, this place is not as bad as that over-priced apartment! The furnace there seldom worked, so we were just as cold, plus, I was always afraid of a serious fire. The gas stove broke down two days ago—for the fourth time in two months—and the manager refused to get it repaired. Then when she kicked us out, she gave us only ten minutes to gather our things!

Art: That's terrible! Where were you living?

Joe: At the Kenton Apartment Complex.

Art's mouth drops open and he stares at the three in horror. Then he drops his head into his hands.

Joe: Are you okay? Did I say something wrong?

Art (*slowly looks up, then speaks softly*): I'm the owner of that apartment complex. You must be Joe and Mary Ann Christian.

Joe: Oh! I—I'm sorry! (*Looks helplessly at* Mary Ann.) Since we've never met, I had no idea who you were.

Art (*voice cracking*): This is absolutely the worst thing I've ever done in my life.

Mary Ann: Mr. Kenton, look at it this way, if we hadn't been evicted, we wouldn't have been here to help you. And you might have—probably would have—died in that terrible storm. I'm *glad* we were here to help you!

Joe (*kindly*): I'd say that God was watching over you tonight.

Art (*nods head slowly*): Yes, (*his voice cracks*) I prayed for help. That's when you appeared out of the darkness, like an angel sent by God. That's the only answer.

Joe: Mr. Kenton, this has become a very special Christmas Eve for all of us. Mary Ann and I might be short on material things (*gestures around the barn*), but we have plenty of God's love in our hearts and tonight we were able to share that with someone less fortunate—I mean, someone who was really in need—I mean—(*looks at* Mary Ann *for help*).

Mary Ann (*laughs kindly*): Well, let's face it Mr. Kenton, you were desperately in need of help!

Art (*sadly, head bowed*): Joe was right when he said "someone less fortunate, someone in need." (*Chokes on words*): Why the good Lord ever saved my life, I'll never know. I certainly don't deserve it. (*Pauses, looks up*): God was working through all three of you. The evidence is *overwhelming*. (*Gestures to Joe*): You, a carpenter named *Joe Christian*, and you (*gestures to Mary Ann*), a woman named *Mary*, giving birth to a baby boy, in a barn, on Christmas Eve! Joe found my car by the light of a star, and we're on Bethlehem Road! (*Smiles wryly.*) I don't suppose you're going to name your baby "Jesus," are you?

Joe and Mary Ann break into gales of laughter—they laugh so hard they cry, while Art looks at them as if they've lost their minds. Finally, Mary Ann gains enough composure to answer Art's question.

Mary Ann: You're never going to believe this, but we decided months ago that if we had a boy, we would name him "Emmanuel," after his grandfather.

Art (*hand to forehead*): I should have guessed! (*Wipes his eyes.*) This has been the most humbling experience of my life. My wife told me just tonight that I should follow the road to Bethlehem—and look what happened when I did! Because of you, my life has been saved—physically and spiritually.

Joe: Mr. Kenton, that shouldn't surprise us. By following the road to Bethlehem, people have been receiving countless blessings for more than 2000 years.

Art (*nods*): Thank God for the road to Bethlehem! (*Goes to Joe and Mary, embraces them.*)

END OF SCENE THREE

SCENE FOUR: *Lights come up on living room scene where Art is still asleep in the position where we left him in scene one. He slowly awakens, then shakes his head as if to clear it, then quickly sits upright.*

Art: Was I dreaming? It was so real! (*Shakes head again*). That had to be more than a dream! (*Looks up, reflecting.*) Thank You, Lord! (*Gets up, walks toward the Christmas tree, then suddenly smacks his hand to his head*): That's amazing! All our family Christmas gifts are things the Christians desperately need: money, a car, a microwave, refrigerator, stove, and a washer-dryer! (*Very excited*): And a new crib! (*Shakes head in disbelief, then looks upward*): *Finally*, Lord, I think I've got Your message! It took a club over my head to get my attention. How can I *ever* repay Joe and Mary Ann? What can I do to help them? (*Quiet, reflecting.*) Shirley and I saw them on that TV special at the Good Samaritan Agency. Lord, forgive me for missing your message then! Please let them still be there! (*Quickly reaches for the telephone, dials, listens.*)

Recorded voice of Bruce: Merry Christmas! This is Bruce at the the Good Samaritan Agency.

Art: Merry Christmas to you, too! This is Art Kenton. Can you tell me if the Joe Christian family is still there?

Bruce: What a coincidence! I have Joe on the other line! He called from the hospital to report the good news that Mary Ann had her baby—can you believe that? *Joe* and *Mary* Ann Christian having a baby boy on Christmas Eve?

Art (*excitedly*): Buddy, you don't know the half of it! They named him "Emmanuel"!

Bruce (*short pause*): That's right. How did you know?

Art (*laughing*): I got the word from higher authority! Listen can you connect us?

Bruce: Sure thing; hold on.

Recorded voice of Joe: Hello, Joe Christian speaking.

Art: Hi, Joe! This is Art Kenton. Congratulations!

Joe (*hesitantly*): I don't believe I know you. Have we met?

Art: No, but I feel as if we have. How's little Emmanuel?

Joe (*short pause*): I don't understand. He was just born a few minutes ago. How did you know about him?

Art: I've got special connections. And how's Mary Ann?

Joe (*guardedly*): Both she and Manny are fine.

Art: Listen Joe, as the owner of Kenton Apartment Complex, I'm the man personally responsible for your problems there.

Joe (*pause, speaks even more guardedly*): I see. I guess I'm surprised to hear that from you. I don't know what to say.

Art: Joe, if I may call you that, I want to ask your forgiveness for the many terrible things I've done to hurt you and Mary Ann.

Joe (*two second silence*): You're forgiven.

Art: Thank you. And I'd like to try to make amends. Can you meet me back at your old apartment tomorrow afternoon?

Joe (*hesitantly*): I . . . I don't know. . . I don't understand.

Art: I want to help you and your family by giving you several things, including a free apartment for as long as you need it!

Joe: But we're total strangers to you, Mr. Kenton. Why would you do such a thing for us? Is this a joke?

Art: You're not a stranger to me at all—you're my brother in Christ! And furthermore, you've had a tremendous impact on my life! Why, I'd count it as a personal blessing if you'd allow me to make amends for the terrible grief I've caused you and your wife!

Joe: You're a Christian brother, huh? Well, since you put it like that. . . I, I guess I'm still a little overwhelmed—are you sure this isn't a joke?

Art (*laughs happily*): You just meet me at the apartment tomorrow at, say, twelve noon, and you'll see how serious I am!

Joe: Well. . . OK, Mr. Kenton. See you then.

Art (*hangs up, looks upward, excitedly*): And from now on, Lord, I promise to *always* follow the road to Bethlehem!

CURTAIN